Acknowledgements

We are grateful to the following for permission to reproduce copyright material:

Bee Research Association for an extract from *Trees and Shrubs valuable to bees;* Botanical Society of the British Isles for an extract from *Code of Conduct* by Botanical Society of the British Isles; British Agrochemicals Association for an extract from *Pesticides: A Code of Conduct* issued by The Joint BAA/Wildlife Education and Communications Committee representing in the United Kingdom: Manufacturers, Distributors and Users of Pesticides, Ministry of Agriculture, Fisheries and Food, Nature Conservancy (National Environment Research Council) Voluntary Conservation Organisations; The author and Devon Trust for Nature Conservation for an extract from *Wildlife Conservation with Dead Wood* Sept. 1972 by Alan Stubbs; Dryad Limited for an adaptation of information from *The Use of Vegetable Dyes* by Violetta Thurstan; Forestry Commission for extracts from *Forestry and the Town School* and other Booklets published by them; The Geographical Association for an extract from *The Botanic Garden in Geography Teaching* by R. H. Thomas; Her Majesty's Stationery Office for extracts from 'Education pamphlet 35'—*Schools and the Countryside;* Monks Wood Experimental Station (The Nature Conservancy) for an extract from *Code for Insect Collecting* by the Joint Committee for the Conservation of British Insects; Northumberland Wildlife Trust for an extract from *'Rescue' European Conservation Year* by the Northumberland Wildlife Trust; Royal Society for the protection of Birds for extracts from Ch. XII 'Farming and Wildlife' from *Farming with Wildlife* and an extract from *Feed the Birds* and International Union for Conservation of Nature and Natural Resources for the environmental curriculum of the Final Report of the meeting at the Foresta Institute.

For permission to reproduce photographs we are grateful to the following:

Aerofilms, page 7; Norman Butler, page 31; Graham Carter, pages 124–125; Civic Trust, pages 34–35, 42–43; Forestry Commission, page 59; Michael Kaufmann, page 4 bottom left, 25, 38 and 134; Longman Group Ltd page 18; Mervyn Rees FRPS, page 107; W. H. Rendell ARPS, pages 19 and 44; Colin Rogers, page 4 top, 4–5 centre, 117 top; All other photographs are courtesy of the authors.

The school outdoor resource area

Schools Council Project Environment
The Schools Council Project
Environment was established
in the University of
Newcastle-upon-Tyne from
April 1970 to August 1973.
The project undertook
research and development in
environmental education for
pupils between the ages of
8 and 18.

Director R. W. Colton
Deputy director R. F. Morgan

Project Environment

The school outdoor resource area

Published for the Schools Council by Longman

**Longman
1724-1974**

Longman Group Limited
London
*Associated companies, branches
and representatives throughout
the world*

© Schools Council Publications
1974

First published 1974

ISBN 0 582 35176 6

Filmset by Photoprint Plates
Limited, Rayleigh, Essex

Printed in Great Britain by
Compton Printing Ltd. Aylesbury

Contents

Introduction

It is accepted that work in schools should move beyond classroom activities to become more closely involved with the world outside. Children now undertake a good deal more fieldwork and are involved in more school visits both in the immediate neighbourhood of the school and at a distance.

No one would wish to belittle the value of fieldwork away from school. No one who has experience of it would deny that there can be difficulties (cost of transport, timetable difficulties, time taken in travel, dependence on weather conditions are some) and there is usually a lack of flexibility which prevents the spontaneous sortie when some teaching situation arises which demands contact with the real thing. The school grounds provide a convenient and ever-present bridge to this outside world. They cannot replace contact with the wider world any more than they can eliminate the need for classrooms and laboratories. They can provide a valuable ingredient in the total education of children comparable to experience within the school building or in the school-time contacts with the wider world.

Sometimes work in the school grounds can be a preliminary or a follow-up or a supplement to a particular classroom activity or out-of-school visit. Sometimes it can offer quite different and new teaching opportunities. Our contention is that the school grounds should be so planned and maintained as to encourage every teacher, whatever his subject, to use them when he feels that this will enliven his teaching. They should become a place which positively invites such activity. All too often they are somewhere where organised games are played and which must be kept tidy, any other use being considered an encroachment on this complacent regime.

The first chapter of this book states the case for using the school grounds in this way. The present rapid growth of the provision of LEA field study centres, both residential and non-residential, is an indication of the trend towards giving children firsthand contact with the countryside and with living things in their natural surroundings.

Much of the value of these centres lies in the unique facilities each offers and the particular interest of its surroundings. A good deal of the learning of general field skills and basic knowledge, particularly about plants and animals and their environment, could be carried out in school grounds. Similarly, experimental and follow-up work from visits could be developed on the school site, so adding to the depth of experience and value of the visit.

Visits cease to become isolated days out and form a cohesive part of the child's education when they are woven into continuing activities using collectively the resources of the field study site, the school estate and the laboratory and other indoor facilities. While the school estate should make provision for all, it is its collections of living material in particular that are likely to be its most used resources. So chapter 2, the main body of the book, deals with provision for the study of living things and their environment. This does not mean that the school estate should not be available as a resource for any aspect of teaching where needed. We deal with what lies in our province and would not presume to trespass elsewhere. Nevertheless, experience has shown that help is most often needed in this direction and that enrichment such as we suggest can be useful to many areas of the curriculum.

Chapter 3 suggests ways in which some of these resources may be provided where the school site is limited and where there is little space for development.

Finally, our work with teachers and LEA officials has made it clear to us that some suggestions are needed about the mechanics of providing and managing the outdoor resource area and about ways in which teachers can find out how to make the most of it. This is the purpose of chapter 4.

Very few outdoor resource areas will contain all the features mentioned, certainly not in their early stages. On the other hand, there are plenty of other directions in which development may occur, according to local conditions and local enterprises and the children's own interests. It is wise not to be too ambitious to begin with but to make a small beginning with a few projects; when it is seen that these can be managed successfully in the time available further development can be started. While one must be prepared to take the long-term view as, for example, in starting a forestry plot, it is essential to maintain enough short-term studies to hold the children's interest.

There are many frustrations to be faced in this sort of work, as any gardener knows—the vagaries of the weather, the attack of pests and diseases, damage caused accidentally by children or maliciously by intruders, and the capriciousness of plant life in itself. But if only some of these can be overcome, another dimension will have been added to the work of the school and the barrier of the classroom walls will have been crossed.

These notes are about an *outdoor* resource area and so they do not deal with laboratory facilities or greenhouses, important as these are to complement outdoor resources. Nor do we deal with the housing and keeping of animals. We know many people will want to have greenhouses and livestock facilities on their estate, but we feel it inappropriate here to deal with such matters as siting and design of buildings and selection of equipment. These require detail which is heavily dependent on local situations and such things as LEA purchasing policy and financial provision. Also there is existing literature on these matters and we see no point in duplicating this.

We have limited ourselves to making out a case for the use of the school estate as an outdoor resource area and suggesting some of the provision that might be made. We have not attempted to say what to teach or how to teach using these resources. A number of existing books on natural history and biology describe how to use some of the school estate features which we mention. Nor have we attempted, generally, to describe how to construct garden features or how to grow plants. Construction and culture are covered in a massive horticultural literature.

Conditions vary enormously from school to school, both in the needs of the children and in the educational potential of the site. So we have not attempted to say what should be the nature or extent of the provision for any group of children, infants or sixth-formers. We have confined ourselves to suggestions which we hope will be useful in a wide variety of circumstances. Poplars grow quickly and oaks slowly whoever is studying them!

A few books are listed which are particularly useful in connection with matters dealt with here. We believe that this very short list will be more useful than a lengthy bibliography. A number of these exist and the Council for Environmental Education publish one which is kept up-to-date by periodic supplements: *Directory of Environmental literature and teaching Aids,* compiled by C. Johnson and J. Smith, obtainable from Council for Environmental Education, c/o School of Education, University of Reading, London Road, Reading RG1 5AG.

1 The value of an outdoor resource area

A new look at the school grounds

In many areas the need for thinking afresh about the design of school buildings, consequent on new ideas about curriculum and organisation, has been recognised and exciting new buildings have been produced. The idea has not been to improve and update traditional workrooms, laboratories and libraries, but to examine afresh the needs of teachers and children working together in the newer, freer situation schools are developing. Libraries are expanding into resource centres which provide audiovisual and programmed learning materials and facilities, practical areas allowing work to ebb and flow between domestic economy, art and handicrafts are being tried instead of compartmentalised specialist rooms and the provision for the sciences is being made more flexible in comparable ways. We need a similar imaginative approach to the provision and use of land surrounding the school so that it will serve the needs of the whole school more fully and so that all teachers can, if they wish, have the opportunity of carrying out some of their teaching outside the classroom. It is hoped that the entire staff would come to regard the whole school site as a matter of concern for them, even though it would be of most use to biologists, geographers, rural studies and environmental science teachers.

In new schools the outdoor resource area can be planned from the outset to fit in with the projected needs of pupils and staff. Existing schools have not this advantage but experience of working with teachers and advisers in many parts of the country has shown that great improvements are often possible, even when there is no chance of acquiring extra land. Pieces of land which are unused or underused have come to light, and where no other space has been found edges and corners of playing fields have been made more interesting and attractive through tree and shrub planting. Ornamental surrounds have been changed to make them more useful for teaching,

plan of an outdoor and domestic science area

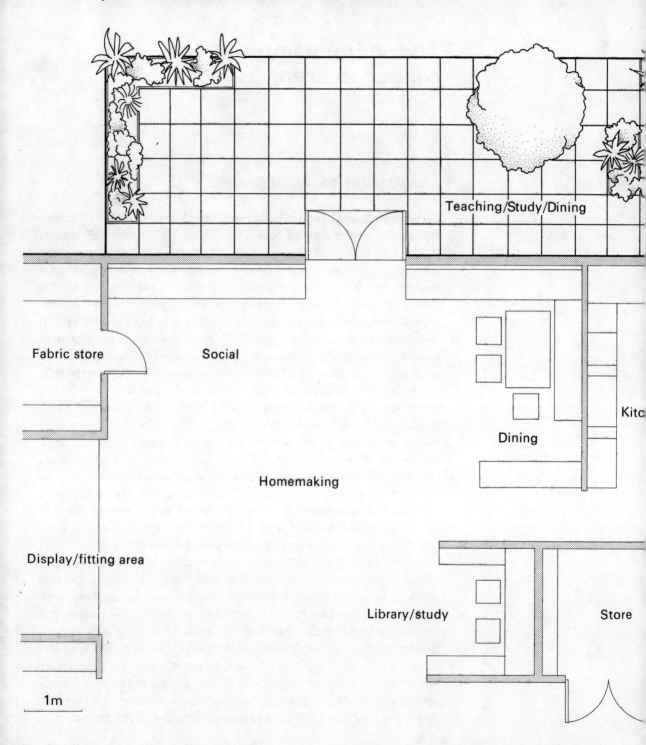

Teaching/Study/Dining

Fabric store

Social

Dining

Kitc

Homemaking

Display/fitting area

Library/study

Store

1m

Herb garden

Dining

Laundry area

Housecraft

Store

a plantation alongside playing fields

mature trees in school

and courtyards have been transformed, even in some cases where this involved breaking up a concrete surface. This has usually been achieved without even the slightest intrusion into playing spaces. Indeed, in the course of our work with some local education authorities irregular-shaped areas, unused courtyards, strips of land between schools and main roads and even pieces of woodland have been discovered, areas which had not been considered for educational use or which the school did not know belonged to the local education authority. The Chief Playing Fields Officer of one large northern county made a quick survey by asking his divisional maintenance officers to recall features on the sites of schools on their lists. This revealed that even in the more industrial divisions many schools have features which could be developed as educational resources. Most abundant were mature trees followed closely by areas variously described as rough land, waste land, copses and wild areas. Only marginally fewer were hedges and tree plantations. Many of the latter were established recently for amenity purposes. There were almost as many streams, brooks and other watercourses which either ran through the site or formed one of its boundaries. A number of the schools had ditches, with occasional flow of water, and others had small areas of mature woodland as opposed to the newer plantations. Finally a few schools had natural ponds or areas of marsh.

a potentially useful area

The present situation

At present when a school is built a certain area of land is set aside for playing field accommodation and for a hard surface area. The minimum areas required for these purposes are set down in the *Standards of School Premises Regulations* issued by the Department of Education and Science (HMSO, 1959; reprinted with amendments 1969). Limited areas around the front and sides of the building, which are of no value for any other use, are set aside for ornamental planting. Some land may or may not be allocated for broader educational uses such as those mentioned in the following pages, but unlike playing field and hard areas, this land is not a statutory requirement under the Standards for School Premises Regulations and may be taken for other purposes without notice. The Regulations need to be revised to extend statutory protection to the full variety of uses to which the school estate may be put.

It is a matter of common observation to those who visit schools that much of the school grounds are unused for most of the time. This is an unsatisfactory situation in a country where land is scarce and expensive and where the population is more crowded than most other countries, even than in one with such a huge population as India. We are frequently and rightly reminded of the need for multiple land use and public institutions such as schools ought to be giving a lead. Seen in this light, schools have a responsibility to use their grounds for the greatest variety of educational purposes. The present view of the school buildings as the teaching area, with some use of the grounds as a playing area, does not fit this concept; this does not make the best educational use of the land given over to schools, nor does it give the public the impression of precious land being used to the maximum advantage. For this to be the case one might expect to see the school grounds used to the fullest extent for a wide range of educational activities. There might also be a conservation area (in the biological, not the legal sense) which ought to be a well planned and attractive feature in the local scene. In fact, the opposite often obtains and the site is deliberately degraded. It is distressing to find that even where educationally useful features (ponds, hedges, copses, waste areas) exist in new school grounds, these are destroyed and levelled to simplify mowing, cheapen maintenance and to provide tidiness. As a result of this simplified-maintenance priority attitude, many acres of potentially educational land resource must be unused and a large number of features of educational value, environmentally desirable and in some cases of historical interest, are irrevocably lost.

One frequently hears education officials and school staff talking of grounds maintenance areas and education areas, the implication being that only the latter areas are available for any educational project school staff or LEA advisers may wish to initiate; the grounds areas are inviolable. Schools ought to be able to use their grounds to the best educational advantage and maintenance ought to be consequent on this, not the determining factor. Maintenance officers say that the shortage of money for any but the simplest form of maintenance is a major problem. Some re-examination of the matter and research into the timing and nature of alternative forms of maintenance to gang-mowing may show that some of these al-

under-used school grounds?

ternatives are equally inexpensive, particularly where they occur in the winter season when labour demand is reduced. A number of playing fields maintenance superintendents already share this view.

Advisers and teachers who depend on outdoor areas on school estates, other than games areas, for their teaching are concerned about the security of their teaching resources. This concern is fully justified by innumerable cases of resources lost in order to provide land for additional building. Even where such useful educational features as school gardens have been created after years of patient effort, it is now common to see them destroyed to make way for new buildings while other areas which have not been so laboriously developed go unscathed. The argument that buildings have priority because gardens are temporary in nature and can be set up elsewhere is fallacious. They are not temporary and their features, particularly those of ecological value, are slow to mature and yield their full potential. We have seen examples of the destruction of gardens which, if replaced, would take ten or twenty or more years to reach an equivalent value educationally, in order to build classrooms which, at most, take a matter of months from foundation laying to yield their full educational potential. Furthermore, a garden usually has been sited from the point of view of the best soil and aspect; replacement usually means a poorer site, though one which might be quite adequate for the erection of a building.

It is essential that in siting new schools and designing the layout of the sites there is a detailed look at possible future needs. When new schools are projected, planning should include the provision of such features as school gardens in positions conveniently close to existing buildings yet safe from possible building extensions. Similarly the future safety of areas for conservation purposes should also be a matter of prime concern. The careful consideration of convenient siting for outdoor resource areas is no less realistic than the arrangement of services and resources spaces in a laboratory and should command the same serious and detailed deliberation.

We frequently hear from local education authority advisers responsible for rural and environmental studies that they are handicapped in pressing for appropriate provision. They complain that while their colleagues dealing with other subjects are able to quote Department of Education and Science advisory publications, they can produce no such support for the school activities for which they are responsible. Land for the purposes mentioned in this publication is not a statutory requirement under the *Standards of Schools Premises Regulations.* While LEAs would not welcome compulsion in these matters it has been suggested to us that they would welcome changes in the regulations that encouraged them to develop school grounds in a more imaginative way.

The use of the school estate

Children of all ages can benefit from school grounds that are imaginatively developed to provide stimulation and facilities for work and also places for quiet enjoyment and relaxation. So, while the range and variety of work made possible by the development of the school grounds may be greater in secondary schools and the area available will usually be much larger, the general principles developed are applicable to all sorts of schools. If the emphasis in this book is biological this is because almost all the people with whom we have talked and worked agree that a varied and attractive school setting with a variety of living things has most to offer. Perhaps nothing else can enhance the school site aesthetically and educationally as much as well conceived plantings of trees and shrubs.

There are many examples up and down the country of the uses to which the school site may be put.

a   An obvious one is that of the rural studies area—usually a garden and livestock unit—which at its best has provided opportunities for all sorts of practical work in realistic conditions. Caring for living things can give children great satisfaction and a feeling of achievement and can be important in developing a sense of responsibility; also there are opportunities for emotional involvement and development of aesthetic sensitivity which may be denied the children elsewhere.

b   The rural studies area has often provided opportunities for a great variety of constructional work—paths, ponds, seats, live-

a rural studies area

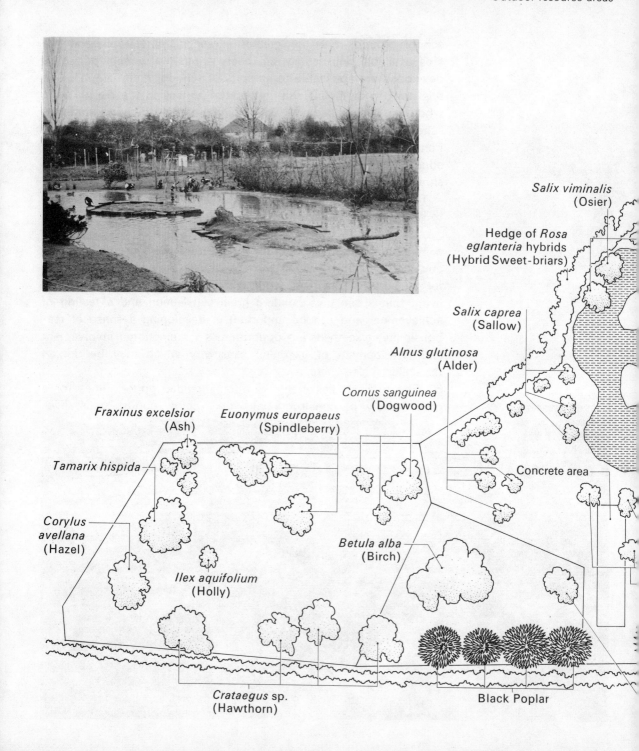

Salix viminalis
(Osier)

Hedge of *Rosa eglanteria* hybrids
(Hybrid Sweet-briars)

Salix caprea
(Sallow)

Alnus glutinosa
(Alder)

Cornus sanguinea
(Dogwood)

Fraxinus excelsior
(Ash)

Euonymus europaeus
(Spindleberry)

Tamarix hispida

Concrete area

Corylus avellana
(Hazel)

Betula alba
(Birch)

Ilex aquifolium
(Holly)

Crataegus sp.
(Hawthorn)

Black Poplar

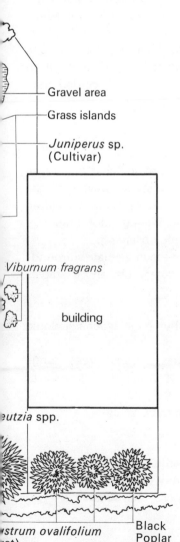

school wildfowl reserve

Gravel area

Grass islands

Juniperus sp.
(Cultivar)

Viburnum fragrans

building

eutzia spp.

*strum ovalifolium
et)*

Black
Poplar

stock buildings, greenhouses, frames, and so on. Here children can feel they are working for an obvious, real-life purpose and not executing some academic exercise.

c   The school garden has long been recognised as an outdoor laboratory. Changes in science teaching, closer collaboration between subject specialists and the development of new environmental syllabuses make the need for such facilities even more important. The new Nuffield A-level Biology, O-level Biology, Combined Science, Secondary Science and the Schools Council/Nuffield 5/13 Science projects all suggest experimental work to be carried out using resources which the school estate could provide; in some cases specific cultivated plots are required. About half the case histories listed by the Nuffield Junior Science project originated outside the classroom, sometimes in the school grounds, sometimes in situations in local parks or waste places which could be reproduced within the school boundaries.

d   In some schools a variety of artificial habitats has been created— bog, heath, rough grassland, deciduous woodlands, ponds, and so on, thus enriching the life to be found on the estate and providing a greater range of material for study. One school has constructed a pond for behavioural studies on wildfowl so making practicable work on the ecological principles of animal behaviour which would otherwise be impossible.

e   Some schools have developed natural areas in the school grounds where wildlife can be studied close at hand. Such provision may be in odd corners of the site, along the margins of playing areas or on some additional area provided for the purpose when the school was built, or specially acquired later. The playing field itself and the lawns may provide opportunities for study of grassland ecology. Some schools have developed nature trails through their grounds. The new impetus to environmental education and the increased interest in ecology which it has brought about make such provision more than ever desirable.

f   Wild areas may be set aside as nature reserves. In at least one local education authority such areas are specifically designated and protected for this purpose. The whole school site could be looked upon as a place where wild things can find refuge. This would demonstrate to the children the school's practical concern with the protection of wildlife.

g   The school estate offers educational opportunities beyond the biologically centred use so far described. Most subject advisers are placing emphasis on moving beyond the walls of the classroom and using the environment outside the school building, either to provide resources for forwarding subject knowledge or as a direct attempt to create environmental awareness through the subject's specialist interest. A rich and well-designed school estate can provide opportunities for most subjects close at hand and without expenditure of time and money on travelling. It would be possible to produce a whole catalogue of instances where various subject teachers make use of some part of the outdoor facilities. For example the following notes give some ideas, for which we are grateful to members of H.M. Inspectorate. We hope we have recorded their views accurately.

Art and craft

Features in school grounds which art teachers would wish to develop
1   Most art teachers do not accept that the studio walls form the natural boundaries of their activities and in many schools children can be found outside the buildings, drawing, filming, photographing, taking rubbings, modelling, carving or simply observing.
2   The requirements of the art teacher from the immediate surroundings of the school seem to fall into three categories, and examples from each are given below.
a   Sources of design
This is by no means an exhaustive list but most teachers would want from the immediate environment:
a variety of natural forms: plant structures, blooms, trees, fungi, pond life, animals, rock or stone forms of structures, varieties of texture, surface pattern and finishes,
Suitable sites for materials to be left to: rust, rot, weather.
b   Materials to work with
Sand pit,
large scale constructional equipment (adventure playground),
wall and floor surfaces suitable for temporary decorative finishes,
waste ground with bricks, Thermolite blocks etc. suitable for kiln building and other structural activity.
c   Appropriate space to work in
Covered sculpture court suitable for carving, construction etc.,

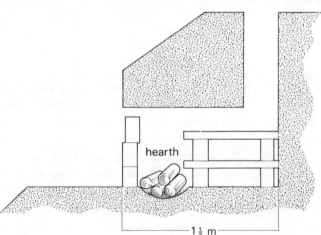

plan of a kiln built
in an earth bank

hearth

1½ m

space for work with large temporary structures such as inflatables,
suitable sites for the display of sculpture, large scale painting,
ceramic, mosaic and other panels and structures,
sites for open air dance/drama/music/art events.

3 These suggestions indicate some of the ways in which art
teachers are at present attempting to use the immediate area outside
the school buildings but the general indication is of a requirement
for open spaces that are both visually stimulating and flexible in use
rather than those with a prescribed function.

Geography

A group of geographers suggest:

. . . an area, safe from vandalism and accessible to pupils, for a weather station including a Stevenson Screen. We also like to have freedom to dig small pits for soil examination and testing. (These could be a couple of feet or more deep depending on the horizons of soil.) Surveying may be taught and it is an advantage if the slopes are not all removed. A patch of 'wild' copse in a corner, or a strip along one side, is a useful thing for geographers as well as biologists.

We have seen, on occasion, large maps of Britain or a continent laid out on the ground on a patch (say 10 m by 10 m) on which pupils can indicate mountains, rivers, railways, roads, and towns. We have also seen large sand-pits for modelling landforms with water laid on to sprinkle rain and cause erosion and deposition.

Home economics

Home economics is, by definition, concerned with the home and environment and if the school grounds are not used as an important resource area, a most valuable teaching and learning opportunity is wasted.

Appreciation and awareness of one's surroundings and a sense of responsibility for their maintenance and improvement are aspects of home economics teaching in which the school grounds can play a vital part.

Management of resources (time, money, space, materials and equipment) is a fundamental part of any home economics course. If the school grounds can be planned to include areas which reflect some of the limitations and/or advantages of the locality, really practical work in such management of resources becomes a possibility. For example on the one hand utilisation of tiny areas of garden, courtyard, balcony, or window-box can be planned and on the other hand, imaginative design and labour-saving planning of larger areas can be considered. The special needs of small children, the economics of food and flower production and the aesthetic possibilities of the environment can all be investigated.

Drama, dance, creative writing and music

The enriched environments found in well designed school grounds offer considerable sensory experience for stimulating and inspiring children to work creatively, for example in poetry and prose to recreate situations and the feelings they arouse which gave rise to literary works by the great naturalist poets and writers and to find a richer world for developing linguistic abilities. Coupled with this richer source of experience is the more free, expansive situation of working out of doors which enables them to find greater freedom of expression through the various art forms. The value of outdoor areas as sites for open air dance, drama, and music events has often been exploited.

Mathematics

Maths in the classroom usually involves limited or secondhand activities with the keystones of mathematics—space and number. By linking the classroom with the whole estate, the opportunities become not only firsthand and real but also extensive. The origins

of maths were in the attempt to understand and order the natural world and there are ample opportunities within the school estate for looking at spatial and numerical relationships. Apart from the obvious measuring and computing, the live and real examples of statistical analysis provide opportunities for study of many of the key mathematical concepts.

Measurement, length and angle

1 Various plots can be mapped to scale in a variety of ways— pacing, using a plane table and taking measurements from a base, using a base line and sighting points (triangulation), using the method of offsets from a base line. Results from a wide variety of methods including methods using other aids of surveying could be compared with advantage. In this way relative approximation could be understood.

2 Heights of buildings and trees could be first estimated then measured using different methods and comparing results.

3 Areas (it is important that problems of this kind should be closely associated with a given problem). For example area of leaves, coverage of tree foliage, area of parts of the field given over to sports.

4 Volume. Two stones of different shape approximately the same size. Which is larger? Which absorbs more water? Which soil sample is most (least) absorbent? Does the size of particle matter? This experiment might well be followed up in the classroom using marbles of different sizes.

5 Statistics. Range of length (width, area) of leaves on a twig, small branch. Distribution of leaf buds (count number of buds between two adjacent buds one vertically above the other on the twig). Study of random samples (quarter of a square metre) of plants on a patch of ground. How many samples are required to give a reasonable picture of the total?

6 Keeping animals. Cost, quantity of food, feeding times. Adult/ child ratio of heights, girths, and of corresponding weights. (This will lead to a study, in the classroom of three-dimensional scale.)

7 Plants. Percentage germination under a variety of conditions of garden plants and wild flowers. Study of symmetry from flowers and leaves.

8 Athletics. Measurement of lengths and times. Comparison with world records (these can be marked out full-scale on the field).

Mark out statistics from the highway code full-scale; braking
distances of cars travelling at different speeds. What is the relation?
9   Study of areas illuminated by artificial lighting of school grounds.
Is this effective? Could it be improved by different placements of
lights?
10   Weather observations. Mathematical use could be made of all
weather observations taken by the geography department. A far
greater attempt could be made to relate observations of different
kinds; for example, wind direction, rain, strength of wind, temperature,
sunshine.

**h   Ministry of Education Pamphlet 35, *Schools and the Countryside*
(HMSO 1958, rep. 1969), offers many suggestions for use of the
countryside by teachers of a number of subjects and many of these
ideas could be followed up in the school estate.**

It [the pamphlet] has three parts. The first deals with three groups
of studies that can be used to illumine the work in three subjects
with a high factual and theoretical content, the second with some
practical subjects especially those which might be included in the
term 'rural subjects', while the third draws attention to the influence
the English countryside has had upon art and literature and, by
implication, suggests a line of further progress. Together, it is hoped
they will provide some new ideas and encourage teachers to use
even more freely the rich source of teaching material to be found in
the countryside.

**j   It would be hard to imagine less stimulating provision for children's
play time in school than the bare, flat exposed tarmac playground
which is all that most schools can offer. A few schools have been
able to develop adventure playgrounds for the younger children. In
these there are grass slopes to climb and roll down, logs, beams and
stepping stones to balance on, trees and frames to climb, pipes to
crawl through, sand pits to play in, ropes and nets to swing on and
other provision for play and construction.**
    Simple ideas are best and sophistication is usually disliked. A
realistic dry land 'boat' can only be a boat whereas a small rough
enclosure can serve perhaps as a boat today and a wild west stage-
coach tomorrow.
    One authority's brief for lower schools states:

It is very desirable that playgrounds are sheltered from the worst of the weather and when possible they should be on the leeward side of the buildings or protected by banks of trees or other means. They should provide for those children who wish to sit quietly in an area set apart from those who wish to play extensively active games.

an adventure playground

k Older children, too, appreciate better outdoor provision than is provided in the majority of schools. In the few schools which have provided seating in an attractive courtyard or lawn setting, the facility has been both appreciated and respected. In an age of noise, crowding and other external pressure upon the individual, opportunities for quiet and for peace are decreasing but nevertheless are equally, if not more, necessary than they ever were. One of the functions of liberal education is to show pupils quality of life and of environment. Architects set out to provide this quality of surroundings when they design the school buildings, especially in generally used spaces

an attractive area for sitting quietly

such as halls and libraries. Wall decorations and furnishings are also chosen to this end. This is most evident when one examines the decoration, curtaining and other furnishings in the main halls and foyers of many of our schools. There is very much less money spent on aesthetic and pleasure-giving features in the school grounds and landscape architects and playing fields officers frequently complain that money for landscaping is taken for contingency costs. Such disparity seems unfortunate if we have in mind the total well-being of pupils.

For both staff and pupils a place outside the building is needed which is comparable with the indoor areas of library and common room, where they can sit and read, relax and enjoy the sunshine and pleasant outdoor surroundings. The cost of such provision is probably less than for many indoor decorative features, judging by the costs of leisure indoor furniture and of curtains and drapes. Well designed surroundings and plantings, once developed, do not need replacement for many years and indeed mature and improve in quality. Similarly paving and lawn, once laid, are permanent. Seating, whether tailormade garden furniture or low capped walling, is less expensive than indoor seating and almost incapable of wearing out.

Few pupils have the incentive or perhaps the opportunity to seek the pleasure of relaxation out of doors in quality surroundings. If for no other reason, schools should provide this opportunity within their estates. Such experiences may awaken our young people to pleasures which they would not otherwise find and might be the stimuli which cause them to improve their future homes and to seek and enjoy the more restful facilities provided in our parks and similar places.

The shortage of field studies facilities

These are times of growing awareness of environmental problems and increasing acceptance by schools that they must play their part in bringing about a responsible attitude in the population. One consequence of this is a rapidly increasing amount of time being spent on studies outside the schools, either in the immediate neighbourhood or at field study centres. But though there has been a considerable increase in the number of these centres, the probability is that the demand will continue to outstrip the provision. There is the danger, too, that areas round some field study sites will become overworked and that the schools themselves may become erosive agents in the countryside. These factors, combined with those of cost, time-tabling difficulties and time spent in getting to and from field study areas, make it imperative to complement work away from the school by work in the school grounds. Many visits to field study sites are spent partially or entirely in learning basic skills and knowledge, so that little time is left for the unique opportunities which the site offers. If, as many educators hope, more and more children under-take visits to field centres or other out-of-school field study sites it will become increasingly important to use these places for their unique possibilities and not to take up time there on teaching the basic skills underlying fieldwork. If the preparatory skills can be learned on the school grounds the fullest use of time can then be made in the field.

The time spent in field studies in distant places is often a dis-parate part of the educational year, not sufficiently connected with the activities of the classroom back at school. Local field activity can build up to the distant visit and on return to school permit follow-up work to blend the visit into the normal flow of work so that both classwork and work away from school form a cohesive whole. So the learning in the classroom and laboratory, local outdoor work and distant studies would fit into a continuous educational pattern. The school outdoor resource area can help to bring about this pattern and also enable children to work outside as and when the need arises, without having to wait for prearranged field trips. For these activities, an area at school no bigger than a football pitch can provide an enormous variety of resources for ecological and other outdoor studies. The area need not necessarily be in one piece; it can be made up of a number of small areas which might otherwise remain unused.

Environmental concern

Our future citizens must be people with a concern for environment. The need for education for the environment is widely accepted now. If we cannot encourage pupils—and teachers—to develop this environmental concern in the surroundings of their school, which provide the day-to-day setting for so much of their lives, then they are unlikely to show much respect for the larger environment. We should show that we care by our treatment and management of the land which forms part of the public provision for education. It is hypocritical to teach about concern for environment while allowing valuable land space in school grounds to remain dreary and un-imaginative in design and barren and poorly managed both from the aesthetic and educational viewpoints.

The *Final Report* of the International Meeting on Environmental Education in the School Curriculum, organised by the International Union for Conservation of Nature in cooperation with UNESCO, (I.U.C.N. Morges, Switzerland 1970), states:

Considering the urgent need for both students and teachers to be in immediate contact with the living natural environment as a necessary basis for an effective environmental education,
Being aware of existing difficulties in making the necessary facilities available, especially in metropolitan areas,
Suggests to Governments, their educational authorities, national educational and conservation organisations, municipal boards and other relevant bodies
1   that appropriate educational nature reserves and natural study areas be made available for use by students and teachers in the process of environmental education.
2   that all schools be provided with their own school gardens and landscape gardens,
3   that all schools be supplied with living teaching materials in cooperation with city park services, forestry services, botanical gardens, nurseries, zoos, etc.,
4   that educational establishments be encouraged or set up to serve the purpose mentioned above.

Some people have seen the suggestion that schools might develop outdoor resource areas as a conflict with the needs of physical education. In fact we see the provision for this subject as part of the overall development of school estates in the best interests of the pupils. The fact that physical education has long used the grounds for pitches and that such provision is a statutory requirement does not detract from the opinion that grounds offer a resource for the total curriculum. Neither does it mean that physical education requirements will not continue to be a major consideration in site planning. What it does imply is an examination of the total site in terms of the whole needs of the children in the school. There is no claim for priority for natural history areas, school gardens or indeed games pitches over other needs. Each has an equal right to outdoor resources and each has special topographical needs. For example, pitches must be laid on level sites of specified sizes, gardens require minimum conditions of soil and aspect. The teacher of physical education can no more teach games on steeply sloping pitches than the biologist can grow plants in poor soil in a sunless position. A balanced appraisal of the grounds of schools as outdoor resource areas is a matter of making the best provision for the whole school which the site will allow and reaching a compromise which offers the best facilities for each of the subject demands.

What we ask for here is not exclusive rights handed to environmental studies or any other curriculum area but the abandonment of selfish subject interests and the development of a cooperative feeling that the whole school is for all its occupants. The design, development and maintenance of the school estate should be approached from the point of view of the educational opportunity for the pupils which it can provide, just as science laboratories, art studios, gymnasia and classrooms are designed with this aim in view. The nature of design which we are suggesting is commensurate with the aesthetic setting for the buildings, which do not necessarily need a background of close-mown, level lawn. Unfortunately, all too often schools are surrounded by these uniformly flat areas of lawn and playing field. Every effort should be made to relieve this monotony.

Planning of sites

Planning departments can make a positive contribution if they understand the nature of schools' needs as regards their surroundings. The clearest and most level site may seem the obvious choice if one is concerned only with the provision of playing fields. If one is looking beyond this to the broader educational possibilities of the school site, one might look for possible land which, in addition to a suitable playing space, offers such features as groups of mature trees, ditches and streams, areas of scrubland, ponds, old railway lines, indeed any features which would give diversity to the outdoor part of the school. Very occasionally the possibility may exist of incorporating some feature of use in studies of archeology or industrial archaeology. Difficult topography which makes the provision of flat areas laborious and expensive is often a help when it comes to planning the site for other purposes.

Naturally enough there have to be adequate flat areas for playing areas, but physical education teachers themselves are often enthusiastic about the improved appearance of their playing fields that results from planting of trees and shrubs and the added shelter they give, provided that these do not encroach on the games areas.

Site planting

Where the selection of tree and shrub subjects has been made with educational use in mind, a valuable resource has been added to schools. Unfortunately, initial planting of sites is often done with little thought for its educational potential. Tree-planting is often limited to a few kinds which are cheap and easily obtained. Where more imagination has been used, and perhaps the school staff consulted, collections of native trees, timber trees and trees with biological interest or associative value, have been built up.

It has been shown that with cooperation between architect, landscape planner, playing fields maintenance staff, LEA advisers and school staff, it is possible to achieve much more extensive, varied and educationally useful initial plantings than is usual. Children's involvement here may give them a greater interest in and concern for the school grounds. Money which might have been spent on contractor's costs has gone towards providing a wider selection of trees and shrubs and the school has seen to the planting of these.

Costs

At a time of rapid inflation it is difficult to suggest realistic figures as cost of land and buildings change rapidly and in addition there are big variations from place to place. It would however be worth comparing outdoor and indoor provision in any given circumstances.

Assume that an area of one fifth of a hectare (say 50 m × 40 m) were set aside for the development of outdoor resources. This is small but it would be useful. Costs vary widely but to take a hypothetical case. Suppose land for a school costs £7 500 per hectare. Our area would then cost £1 500. With building costs at over £120 per square metre, this would cost about the same as a 4 m × 3 m storeroom. What a wealth of educational material would be in this outdoor storeroom, most of it provided free. Furthermore, there would be no depreciation; quite the contrary, for year by year as the trees and shrubs developed and matured they would become a more attractive feature in the school grounds, and the area would increase in educational value as the richness of its wildlife resources increased. In urban areas land would cost much more, but the value of the facility would rise in proportion to its distance from the countryside; it might cost more but it would be infinitely more precious to the school. Where land costs are highest the argument for making the utmost use of such a costly resource is strongest.

One education officer in an area with very high land costs has pointed out that sites often include areas which have to be bought with the rest of the school grounds even though, because of their shape, they are of no value as playing space. He also has said that whenever possible his authority buys in areas of woodland and similar land adjacent to a site it is already purchasing.

Cooperation between schools on campuses

The campus system with an estate common to several schools is not uncommon and it allows for cooperation in development and use. While there may be some disadvantages, such as having to consider other schools in planning for one's own needs, it does provide for helpful and constructive collaboration. Thus the primary school can achieve a richer resource through the activities of the secondary school, while the secondary school gains from the extra space and the occasional use of primary-oriented features as such use becomes appropriate. Further, many primary children would welcome opportunities for realistic and purposeful work which assistance and cooperation with the secondary school could bring. There is too little precedent for such cooperation but it is beginning in such widely differing situations as a comprehensive/junior school campus in a country district and secondary modern girls'/junior/infant/nursery school campus based in a barracklike building set in an extensive brickwalled and tarmac yard. In the latter case the teachers of the four schools met together to set up a steering committee to develop the school yard by importing soil for beds on the tarmac and by setting up container gardens and animals houses. In another case, two schools, one middle and the other secondary, share a garden and school farm area which lies between them.

Too often such areas are divided up into separate school sites. This is a great pity for in most situations the whole can be greater than the sum of the two parts. Where such separation has already taken place, it should be possible to rethink the situation and the potential resource which it offers and to remove the boundary fence to allow resources to be shared where this seems desirable to the teachers involved.

The problem of maintenance

Whenever discussions begin about using school estates for educational purposes the problem of maintenance is raised. In our view, and from our own experience in schools, this problem is grossly overrated, except where school gardens are kept for fund raising or show pieces, which is hardly their proper function. In the first place, the greater part of the estate could comprise natural, informal features. By their nature these require little regular maintenance: no hoeing, digging, grass edge cutting, hedge trimming; at most, such areas require a once-a-year trimming of wayward growth or removal of precocious material to allow a less vigorous plant to develop.

Our school grounds are sometimes referred to as green deserts. What an indictment that is! The excuse usually given is that everything must be arranged to simplify gang mowing and cut costs. It is possible, as farmers are showing, to plan what for the sake of brevity we may call amenity areas along the sides and edges of fields without seriously affecting operating costs. Farmers are being asked to consider wildlife conservation in the management of their farms and the Ministry of Agriculture is supporting this policy. To some extent those responsible for maintaining school playing fields are in a similar position to the farmers. They have to manage the land as effectively as possible with the minimum cost. If farmers, who are in business to make profits, can afford to make provision for wildlife, it seems reasonable to expect public authorities to take a similarly enlightened view in their land management. There is all the more reason for this in the case of school grounds for protection of wildlife here would not be an end in itself but would be a way of providing a unique educational resource.

The Farming and Wildlife Advisory Group have published a leaflet *Farming with Wildlife* which makes certain recommendations about the conservation of wildlife in farms. They say 'Need we continue to regard small parcels of rough land as an affront to good husbandry? On most farms there are areas, perhaps quite small, particularly

a field corner

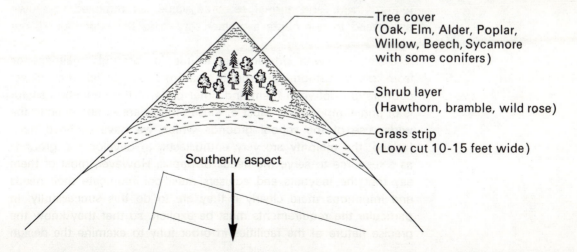

Tree cover
(Oak, Elm, Alder, Poplar,
Willow, Beech, Sycamore
with some conifers)

Shrub layer
(Hawthorn, bramble, wild rose)

Grass strip
(Low cut 10-15 feet wide)

Southerly aspect

valuable for wildlife and deserving of special treatment.' Fuller reference to this leaflet are given, with further extracts in chapter 2 under The school wildlife area (p. 45) and in the diagram on p. 27.

As traditional school estate maintenance is based chiefly on gang mowing, there is need for some new thinking about the role of maintenance teams when school estates become educational resource areas rather than maintenance areas. Because existing maintenance is geared to, and costed on, gang mowing there has been little research or experience with other forms of maintenance. It is too easy to fall back on the fact that over the years time and motion studies have reduced considerably the costs of gang mowing and to claim that this is the only economic form of maintenance.

We have been told by maintenance officers that wintertime, when no mowing is required, is a slack time for labour. Some officers have suggested that features such as informal hedges, which require attention only in winter, would present no labour problem. Many of the features we describe in chapter 2, such as trees, shrubs and much of the wildlife area, require maintenance such as trimming and tidying only in the slack labour period of winter; indeed summer attention would be harmful to their wildlife value because of the disturbance it would cause to plants and animals.

Our talks with maintenance officers, many of whom are conservationists, show that they are concerned about the green deserts they are creating. We believe many would welcome opportunities and encouragement to carry out research into the costs, of both time and money, and into the expertise required in maintenance of features with educational resource value, as opposed to mown areas, and to contribute a greater service to the education of our pupils.

Discussion with officers responsible for grounds maintenance from many authorities strongly reaffirms our belief that closer cooperation between them and other parts of the education sector is of prime importance. Most of these officers are sympathetic to the wider use of the school grounds which we have outlined here. Indeed, the majority are very enthusiastic to develop the grounds as a resource to serve the needs of pupils. However, most of them say that the teachers and advisers must communicate their needs and intentions more clearly if they are to do this successfully. In particular the requirements must be explicit, so that they know the precise nature of the facilities in order fully to examine the design and maintenance involved. They also look for reassurance that the features will have some degree of permanent use and will not be suddenly abandoned. Nearly all say that in the past they have experienced circumstances where, having helped an enthusiastic teacher to develop and maintain a school garden or other teaching resource, that teacher has moved on to another post, his successor has shown no interest in the resource and the grounds staff have been left to maintain something which is no longer used in the children's studies. The first problem will be met as teachers and advisers discover the type of facilities which are most useful to them and are able to explain their needs in precise terms. The second will be satisfied as more and more teachers come to appreciate the valuable support for their teaching and the motivation for their pupils which working out of doors offers. Both the definition of the needs of teachers and pupils and the regular and continuous use of outdoor resources will depend for development upon research and training within the teaching profession. As explained elsewhere initial and in-service training for teachers in the use of resources in school grounds is of paramount importance.

Community use of school grounds

A city authority, planning to develop schools as community centres makes the following points:

It is important as we see it to ensure that parents get a feeling of welcome particularly at our lower schools and every effort is being made to involve and interest parents in the activities that go on there. We hope that the time when parents stay outside the school gate to wait for their children at the end of school has gone. Every encouragement should be given to them to come into the school and sit in the grounds especially on the seats which are being provided round the adventure play areas. Parents should be able to sit and talk with each other and keep an eye on the activities of the younger children not yet of school age who may be with them and who should be allowed to play on the apparatus which has been provided in the form of sand-pits, tree trunks or simple balance bars all unsophisticated but safe.

We appreciate that there are risks involved in integrating a school into a community to this extent. We are trying for instance, to avoid fencing playing fields and wherever possible we are endeavouring to merge the school grounds into some other neighbourhood feature such as a park, a play area or a wood. This will mean that many school facilities will be available to the community and it may be necessary that some form of supervision in the form of a play leader will be necessary in the case of lower and middle schools. In the case of upper schools we hope that there will be a public awareness of what we are endeavouring to achieve and although there is no doubt that we shall suffer many disappointments we hope that in the end we shall win through.

This attitude to the school grounds will be seen as a serious threat to their plans by many teachers who wish to develop them on the lines suggested elsewhere in this book. No doubt it will increase the risk of interference and make it necessary to take special steps to protect particularly vulnerable places. Nevertheless, if the type of community involvement which this city authority seeks can be developed it is likely to be the surest safeguard against vandalism.

The problem of vandalism

The vandal is a problem in many places and outdoor resource areas are obviously very vulnerable. There is no clearcut defined answer, though we describe in a later section some steps which may be taken to ameliorate the situation. The important point is that we must bring up children to understand and respect their surroundings, and involvement with them in school is one way of doing this.

Suggestions for a resource area

A great deal of this book is taken up with suggestions for making the school grounds a home for plants and animals and it may seem that the biological matters have taken up a disproportionate amount of space. However, it has become obvious from our discussions with people interested in using the school grounds as a resource in teaching a variety of subjects that living things can be used to enrich the teaching of many subjects.

The site

Area

How much land do we need? It is impossible to generalise on this question. It all depends upon particular local needs and resources. While the requirements of games are stringent in that pitches must be rectangular, level and unobstructed, and while the regulation size of pitches determines the playing field areas, the outdoor resource area is more flexible in its requirements and more frugal in its space demands. Provision of land for this latter purpose is simpler and less costly in that most available land can be adapted and developed cheaply without extensive levelling, draining and general redevelopment. It is a case of making the best use of whatever local provision can be offered, rather than demanding a universally agreed specification. Obviously the richer the area and, within reason, the larger the space, the greater the potential will be for pupils' education.

In general the natural area can be as big as possible since it involves comparatively little maintenance, but the bigger the site the greater the resources it offers and the better the chance of attracting less common forms of wildlife. It also means that the site will stand more intensive use, and perhaps collecting, without becoming denuded. This does not mean that the tiny corner is to be despised where this is all that is available, indeed on some school sites there may not be one natural area but several small pieces of land situated in corners and along the perimeter.

On the other hand, cultivated areas need to be kept to the minimum that is strictly necessary for the work envisaged. In the past the mistake was often made of planning a range of features, all of which were quite justifiable on educational grounds, and then trying to teach from them. What we ought to do is to decide what we want to teach, what sorts of plants and how many we need to grow to achieve this aim and then provide the space for this. Only in this way can we ensure that our cultivated ground will be used to the fullest extent and that routine maintenance will be kept to the minimum. After all, when we order laboratory equipment we buy the items we require for achieving our teaching objectives, we do not order a variety and then try to arrange our syllabuses around them!

In the initial stages it is as well to have any area intended for cultivation grassed down so that maintenance is reduced to mowing.

informally and formally
cultivated areas

Plots for cultivation can be cut as teaching activities make them necessary. Later on it is as well to be prepared to grass-down plots which no longer have a teaching value rather than have to maintain superfluous cultivated areas. It is necessary, of course, to try to visualise the garden as a whole when developing it in this way, and not to allow it to become a hotchpotch of plots.

Since the whole of the school grounds are a potential educational resource the planting and development of features should be seen in relation to the whole area rather than as plots within the grounds. Nevertheless, just as some part will be needed as a playing area there will be occasions when it will be most convenient to concentrate on a number of features in one small area, for example, a wild area or a place for cultivation or an area designed primarily for nature study.

Situation

Sometimes there will be little choice about where particular features may be sited, but where choice does exist there will usually have to be a compromise between two opposing requirements, seclusion to

encourage wild creatures and proximity to the classroom for ease of access and observation. Sometimes this difficulty may be settled by having a cultivated area near the classroom and a separate wild life area further away. Where one piece of land only is available, it might be wise to follow the old landscape gardening rule and put the more controlled, humanised part of the plot near the buildings and let this lead into the natural area. Quite often, especially in primary schools, there is room for a small school garden near the buildings and natural areas have to be provided around the edges and in the corners of the playing field. We have argued that the two uses ought to be considered together when the site is first laid out, so that both receive fair consideration. However, where it is too late to do this, it is still possible to make good use of leftover spaces.

While we deprecate the situation that all too often obtains in which ease of mowing comes first and educational considerations second, it is only reasonable to see that the areas set aside for outside studies do not make grounds maintenance more difficult. On irregular and sloping sites it is often possible to make a positive contribution by using awkward corners, steep slopes and cut-away areas which mowers cannot reach, for developing resource areas.

It is heartening to find that some local education authorities are appointing landscape architects to advise on the landscaping of school grounds. Consultations, involving their expertise and that of teachers and other educationists, could result in rich educational resource areas designed in the best way aesthetically and in terms of management and maintenance.

Aspect

Where there is some choice in the matter an open sunny site is desirable. It is not difficult then to arrange for shady areas where they are needed but there is not much one can do about getting sunshine to a shady site.

Services

An outside tap or standpipe is a useful facility in a cultivated area and for filling ponds etc. Likewise a waterproof mains socket enabling the use of soil warming cables in frames or cloches and other electrical apparatus to be used outside is desirable. The need for the greatest care in using mains voltages in moist surroundings cannot be overstressed. Such service points require a secure locking device to prevent tampering by vandals, either by being placed within a strong metal box, or by being set below ground under a locked manhole cover. For water such an underground point will avoid loss of supply or damage to the installation through freezing.

Flexibility

We live in a changing world and no part of it changes more than ideas in education. Our present ideas will certainly be considered out-of-date in a few years' time. The whole schools system is undergoing reorganisation, there are great changes in curricula and sweeping changes in examinations may appear. Above all, the outside world changes, and with it the demands of society for the contribution of its schools. So plans ought to be made to allow for as much flexibility as possible where any constructional work is to be done. If one is planting a miniature oakwood or any other purely natural feature, obviously one has to look to the future and hope for some stability in this area, but elsewhere one must expect present ideas to lose their value and new demands to be made. If we are to be free to adapt to these changes we ought not to do anything in our planning which will make alteration difficult. A large concrete pond may fix a garden plan where a plastic one might fulfil the same purpose and yet allow of easy changes when these become desirable. Similarly concrete slabs give firm dry paved areas which can be easily changed whereas *in situ* concrete cannot.

Maintenance

It is the cultivated areas which require the most maintenance. However, even this is not excessive if the areas are planned for their educational value and the features are designed to be labour-saving. School gardens of the traditional 'crop and show' type are the antithesis of this. The most important thing is that the cultivated area be kept to the very minimum consistent with the learning that is intended. If maintenance takes up so much time that there is none left to enjoy and discuss what has been going on, the whole thing is a waste of time. Many schools have found the most satisfactory way of starting is to grass the whole area and only dig up the very smallest part of this to begin with. If this proves inadequate more can be cultivated, but one is not confronted by great weedy tracts waiting to be dealt with. The principle is to provide only for the needs of the pupils. If they want to grow a variety of types of beans to compare their growth they do not need several rows of each; probably half a dozen plants of each will be sufficient.

The maintenance for this exercise does not involve extensive weeding of rows by hand, frequent hoeing and the erecting of rows of bean sticks. The small area involved can be maintained almost incidentally to observing the growth and without any drudgery by the pupils growing the plants. Such minimal maintenance of *their* plants on *their* plot is not asking too much of any pupils be they primary school children growing a few radishes or sixth form biologists growing a few peas and onions from seed to observe the effect of gibberellin on germination and subsequent development. Finally where pupils are to maintain cultivated areas it is as well to remember that schools are in session for only forty weeks of the year. The heavy, continuous maintenance needed by large plots could not be easily fitted into this period even if it were educationally acceptable particularly if long periods of bad weather coincided with it. We have to recognise that school gardening has to be managed within a shortened year, unlike gardening in other spheres.

More permanent features of the cultivated area, for example paths and edges, are always a maintenance problem unless one seeks designs which are labour-saving. For example, cultivated plots with grass edges, even edges lined with metal strip, require constant trimming with shears and often become damaged and need cutting back. Similarly, edging of bricks or stones prevent mowing right to the margin and leave grass which requires cutting with shears. If plots are edged with paving slabs—45 by 45 cm is a convenient size—set to appear flush with the grass (for this they should be about 10 mm below grass level), there is no edge needing trimming and the mower can ride over the slabs and cut all the grass. Furthermore, the slabs provide a serviceable path, requiring no maintenance whatsoever. If it becomes necessary to lift the path and move it elsewhere, this can be done without loss of material.

Much labour on maintenance is caused by using ground which is heavily infested with perennial weeds. It is almost impossible to

corners designed to avoid
wear

clean perennial weeds from between growing crops and it is
worth cleaning infested ground thoroughly by fallowing and
turning the soil frequently before using it for a cultivated area, or
even before grassing down as an area to be cut into later for plots.

The principle of labour-saving edging and clean ground applies
equally to other features such as trees or groups of shrubs or other
plants set in mown grass. Ground well cleaned before planting,
followed by dense planting (removing individuals later as the
plants develop) will take care of most of the weeding maintenance.
Edging the group planting with paving set flush with the grass
solves the edging problem; in many cases growth from the plants
will encroach over the paving after a while and 'soften' the edges.
Similarly, to set some paving flush with the grass around a tree
will permit complete mowing without a collar of unmown grass and
will also prevent damage to the tree from attempts to mow right
up to it.

Neighbours

We must be good neighbours. Even if the education reasons are impeccable we will have to be careful to see that no nuisance is created. A wild area is highly desirable educationally, but to those who live nearby, and who are not aware of the reasons for its existence, some features may seem to be no more than a case of sheer neglect. A good screen of trees or shrubs is therefore desirable in such cases. It may be necessary for our purposes to let docks and thistles go to seed. We ought to see that the numbers involved are no more than necessary and that the risk of seeding into nearby gardens is avoided. Our wild area ought not to be a neglected area and such things as clear pathways, neat labels, tidy boundaries, where appropriate, will help to make it clear that this is not so. Above all, it is a matter of careful siting so that less attractive resource features are screened by others and do not offend our neighbours.

Vandalism

Vandalism is a growing problem in both rural and urban areas. It appears to indicate social malady through boredom and a lack of understanding of other people's needs and of the slow development of living things. Perhaps involvement with a living, changing school estate may do something to bring about this understanding in pupils. There is certainly some experience which suggests that where children are closely involved with a project, they are not destructive towards it; on the contrary, they are the best protective force for it.

Experience shows that where involvement includes making decisions as well as carrying out the work, the children identify closely with the project and value it deeply; it becomes *theirs* and not 'the school's'. So the first step to combat vandalism appears to be to involve the whole school population with the school estate. This is no easy matter, but if the estate becomes a source of real, meaningful, and hence interesting, studies, the pupils will feel a proprietary right in its development and will not only respect it but become custodians against others who may have intentions of vandalism. The results of such an attempt are long-term, but the earlier it begins and the more extensively the estate features in activities at all levels and in all subjects, the sooner will the pupils develop this interest.

More immediately, some preventive steps can be taken to alleviate the problem. The obvious step is to make entry difficult and schools are fortunate which have a caretaker's house on the site. Glasshouses may be glazed with fibreglass or polycarbonate and while these substitutes may not be looked on with favour by glasshouse crop specialists it has to be borne in mind that it is not our aim to produce the best possible crops. We have to make some plants available in difficult conditions.

Vandalism in the strict sense involves wilful destruction, but theft is often the motive of intruders. Planning to avoid temptation to thieve is a wise step. Small apparatus (such as thermometers), vegetables and fruit, poultry and eggs, are all attractive to the thief. Similarly, the presence of other livestock, formally designed garden features, weather-recording apparatus, bird hides and other obvious features attract the attention of wilful destroyers. In areas with much vandalism emphasis on natural features may be helpful.

The greatest problem is in areas of intense vandalism, where any new feature, be it a planted tree, an area of new-sown grass seed or even an empty plant tub, is immediately destroyed. Here the only resort is to physical protection with high link fencing round vulnerable features, though it is both expensive and ugly. Even so, damage will undoubtedly occur. Parks and planning departments have found that sometimes they can succeed by matching the vandal's determination and, for example, by replanting damaged trees again and again. One city school has overcome vandalism to its plants by growing spring bulbs in wooden tubs and bringing them into the school at the end of each afternoon!

There is no quick answer to vandalism. Its effects sap not only the school's resources for replacement but also the spirit of busy teachers. While some limited local attempts at protection or vandal-proof design may help, the real answer lies in the longer-term concern for the school estate by pupils and eventually the community.

The dual nature of the area

It is convenient to think of the value of the outdoor resource area from two points of view, which is not to suggest for one moment that the alternatives are distinct. Classroom work may lead to the need for investigation outside which will in its turn demand follow-up and recording inside.

A place for study outside the classroom

The school grounds can offer opportunities for a range of activities which can only be carried on outside—ecological investigation, wildlife observation, gardening, scientific field trials, weather studies and so on. This is developed further elsewhere. The point to be made here is that the resource area will have to be planned with these activities in mind, considering not only the qualitative but also the quantitative aspects. 'How many?' and 'How often?' in terms of children's use will clearly be important design factors in the grounds.

A source of material for use inside the classroom

The second category is exemplified by the 'supply of biological specimens'—all sorts of material, twigs, leaves, flowers, worms, soil samples and so on. Even if there is countryside around where these can be collected, we must always consider nowadays whether we ought to collect. (There is a strong body of opinion which puts a ban on all collecting by schools in the countryside unless the things being collected are plentiful. Other opinion puts a total ban on collecting on the basis that teachers and pupils do not always know what is plentiful—organisms plentiful in a small area may be rare in the wider ecosystem.)

The outdoor resource area can also supply food plants for laboratory animals, silkmoths, stick insects and locusts, for example, or plants to make vegetable dyes. If we can produce our own, so much the better for we are in a position to control supply and demand and to use such control as an object lesson in conservation.

School grounds as an example of land use and environmental management

It could be a useful experience for children to examine the school grounds as an example of the use of land, as a setting for the school and as part of the local environment as seen by the community.

Questions they may explore include:

Is the land used effectively, that is, is it of the greatest possible benefit to the school?
If not how could it be used to greater advantage?
Is it used intensively or are parts of it unused for long periods?
Is it possible to compare intensity of use with that of local parks or sportsgrounds? Alternatively, how many homes would it provide, given the housing density of local estates?
Does it provide an attractive setting for the school?
Is it a pleasant feature in the neighbourhood?
If it fails in either of these respects what could be done to improve the situation?

Ecology of land management

The grounds might also be developed to show examples of the way in which man uses other organisms and of those which harm these endeavours. There would not be much point in producing a mere catalogue of species but there would be plenty of opportunity to look into the factors affecting the status of the various organisms in their relation to human interests. We might distinguish:

1   Useful organisms

in the school garden, crops which are harvested and used,
in the school garden and surrounds, plants, large and small, which
are grown for their beauty of flower, foliage, form or colour. Flower
beds, trees, shrubs and grass,

a screen of
plants

plants used as screens to hide unsightly places,
plants which have other uses, for example, playing surfaces,
plants used for shelter, to stabilise soil or to provide physical barriers
like hedges,
plants used to encourage animals in nature reserves,
animals which are directly useful, for example, poultry,
animals which are kept or encouraged for interest or beauty, for
example, pet animals, wild birds, butterflies,
animals which are beneficial in a less obvious way, for example,
pollinating insects and those which are parasites or predators on
pests.

2 Other beneficial organisms

Organisms which are indirectly useful as scavengers, decomposers
and for the part they play in maintaining soil fertility.

3 Plants which are unwelcome

because they are unsightly—weeds of lawns, flower beds, etc.,
because they compete with crops—arable weeds,

because they are hosts for pests and diseases,
because they cause structural damage, for example, poplar roots in drains, and weeds lifting asphalt surfaces of paths,
because they cause plant diseases.

4   Animals which harm man or his crops or stock

rats, mice, mosquitoes, etc.,
pests of animals, for example, mites on poultry,
plant pests.

There will also be organisms which do not fit easily into categories of friend or foe because their activities are obscure, or because they are both harmful and beneficial on occasion.

Studying all these organisms might involve trying to find answers to such questions as: How did they come to be there? How are they exploited? How are the useful ones managed? How are the harmful ones controlled? How do they interact? What effect does increase or decrease of one have on the others?

Project Environment's *Production Ecology* (Longman 1975) deals with topics such as these.

The school wildlife area

One function of the school grounds should be to serve as a nature reserve, not necessarily one in which all plants and animals are rigorously preserved but where wildflowers and weeds can be allowed to flourish, where small creatures will be found and where birds can live unmolested. Any other attitude to wildlife on the school site is unthinkable. The actual value of the site as a wildlife refuge might be small though not negligible, particularly if the grounds include more than playing field space, but it would be the example of thoughtful use of environment that would matter. This could be one way in which children came to realise that the school as an organisation cared about these things in a real and practical way and did more than pay lip-service to such principles. This realisation would be reinforced by the conservationist approach to the use of the grounds for their educational resource value. Thus collecting of specimens would be carried out thoughtfully and not in a spirit of exploitation. As suggested in Chapter 4, a specific wildlife or nature reserve management committee comprising pupils, staff and experts from the wider community, supported by the school's own conservation corps, could do much to enrich and improve the range of wildlife, *both* plant and animal, within the grounds.

Positive steps would be taken to encourage wildlife by:

---

setting aside wild or semi-wild areas,
planting for interest and for the benefit of wild creatures as well as for appearance,
providing extra food and shelter in the forms of nest boxes, bird tables etc.,
planting flower borders to attract butterflies and other insects,
judiciously introducing wild species where appropriate and ecologically acceptable.

The whole site would at the same time develop into a wildlife area, attracting wild species irrespective of the formal or informal nature of the individual facilities. Provision would have to be made for planned study while specific areas would have to be protected from intrusion by people, domestic animals, mowers, and so on. Other areas could be set aside for specific investigation of both biotic and abiotic environmental factors.

The ways in which provision can be made will vary enormously from school to school. Broadly speaking, we might distinguish the school which is able to supplement its grounds by a wildlife area away from the site; the school where a specific area can be set aside for the purpose; and the school which makes use of various odd corners and edges.

The following notes taken from the leaflet *Farming with Wildlife* are relevant here. This leaflet is reprinted from *Farming and Wildlife* (ch. xii), edited by D. Barber for the Royal Society for the Protection of Birds in association with the Farming and Wildlife Advisory Group, 1970.

The following suggestions provide some guidance as to what farmers can do in the interests of wildlife and landscape on their farms.

General

1   Have a thought about the future before making too dramatic an impression on those hedges, ponds, and wet places, bits of scrub and the odd trees and spinneys. Anyone who knows anything about farming appreciates the economic pressures that force farmers into intensifying and making use of every bit of land. But it may take thirty years or more for the farm landscape to recover from the blitz to which you subject it when, perhaps as a new entrant to an expensive farm, you are anxious to make every acre pay its way. In a few years when the farm is on an even keel you may regret the treeless, hedgeless prairie view from the farmhouse windows.

2   Do check up on your calculations before sending in the bull-dozer. It's not just that these bits of woodland or gorse or ponds provide habitats for butterflies and birds; we need them to maintain a proper balance in the countryside between everything that lives there, including ourselves.

3   Keep hedge trimming to the autumn and winter to avoid nesting birds; if this can be done on a two or three year cycle, it will allow shrubs to have flowers and berries and will benefit many insects.

Hedges

1   The hedge which carries the greatest abundance and variety of wildlife is the tall unkempt hedge with a thick ground cover at the base. Unfortunately, this hedge can be expensive to maintain.

2   The oldest hedges on the farm will be the richest in plant species and these are likely to be the hedges along the farm or parish boundaries or along the roadside. Could perhaps the boundary or roadside hedges be managed a little more sympathetically?

3   And is it necessary to burn or spray all the hedge bottoms annually?

Trees

1   It's not much good suggesting that too much hedgerow timber can be spared in these days of mechanical hedge cutting and dear and scarce labour. But if saplings are near the end of a hedgerow, they might be avoided without undue difficulty. Not only will they give variety to the landscape but they provide an important habitat for wildlife.

2   Unploughed field corners which are expensive and difficult to

cultivate with modern machinery can be useful for wildlife. They can be allowed to colonise naturally or can be planted. But they need to be planted with the right species and there needs to be some variety in each planting.

3   Dead trees are also valuable for wildlife and a remarkable proportion of the British fauna is dependent in some way on dead wood. In certain commercial forestry operations removal of dead trees is necessary but in farm copses they can usually be left with great benefit to wildlife.

4   The best layout for a big field corner would be a grass layer on the outside and a shrub layer, which is particularly important for most species of small birds, surrounding the trees. Hawthorn, bramble, privet and blackthorn are especially useful in the shrub layer and a patch or two of nettles is valuable for butterflies.

The diagram on page 27 provides a useful guide.

5   The best species for wildlife is undoubtedly the English oak, but it is slow growing and should be planted in a mixture with perhaps birch and rowan. The oak provides the most cover for insects and thus, with the acorns, a good food supply for birds. Elm, alder, willow, black and white poplar are some other useful trees.

Water and wet places

1   The cleaning out of watercourses usually leaves a considerable scar on the landscape. If some of the natural vegetation can be left, the reeds, rushes and the like, this will lessen the harmful effects on wildlife and, if planned judiciously, will do little to impede water flow.

2   Areas of wet boggy land are very valuable for plants, insects and birds.

3   Farm ponds, if properly fenced, are often of considerable wildlife interest. A little inexpensive dredging to provide some open water will make a pond more attractive for dragonflies, and other water insects, frogs, and depending on the size, some birds. Shading by trees, however, particularly on the south side, will decrease the interest.

Trees planted

Holly

Scot's Pine

Rowan

Guelder rose

Purging buckthorn
Yew

Hazel

Holly

Spindle
Ash
Field Maple

S.L. Lime

Hazel

Gean

Hazel

Crab Apple, Hazel,
Wych elm
Goat Willow
Aspen Alder
Alder Buckthorn
Bird cherry
Blackthorn thicket

Holly

Guelder rose
Holly

Pesticides

1   Most people do not appreciate that herbicides and insecticides must be used for efficient economic farming and are not always directly toxic to wildlife. However, 'weeds' are plants and many, if not all, provide food and shelter for animals of many sorts.

One of the problems with wildlife areas on school sites, whether based on pre-existing features or developed by planned landscaping and planting, is their vulnerability to future planning. Such apparently unused areas are frequently taken as sites for new buildings. In particular, potential school nature reserves in the form of existing pieces of scrubland, ponds or banks are often destroyed and levelled for ease of ground maintenance when the landscaping of the grounds is being done after new schools are built. On architects' plans, such features seem obvious places for levelling or use for new buildings, because there is nothing to mark them as of special educational value.

Some officials may not be aware of the slow development of these areas and do not realise that the result of many years of natural development is being destroyed and that only many more years can replace it. Thus it is necessary to highlight and to document the importance of such places. This may be done by declaring them nature reserves and drawing up comprehensive development and management plans for them. If this is done by a competent management committee, and if the help of the County Naturalists' Trust is sought in preparing the plans, they will be founded on expert opinion. The Trust brings the children in contact with an outside conservation body; it links the school with the adult world and children may be encouraged to join the organisation and so continue and expand this contact when they leave school.

While such a step carries no legal protection for the site, it does put the reserve on a documented, planned and well-founded footing which is more likely to command attention in any future planning scheme than verbal complaint that a teaching resource is being lost. To strengthen the impact it would be advisable to lodge copies

Established trees

○ Oak	▲ Hawthorn
△ Birch	■ Elder
□ Willow	● Sweet Chestnut
	◊ Lombardy Poplar

additional planting to enrich the school nature reserve (see pages 75–6) of the declaration that the site is a nature reserve and of the management plan with the local education authority and the authority's architect's and planning department. One County Adviser for Environmental Studies, who already works on these lines writes:

School nature reserves have been developed in this county in the last year or so.

The reserves at present are usually areas within the school estates which are fenced off in some way to prevent undue access. In one case this is a six acre wood and in another case a half acre of scruffy untouched turf.

Some schools have reserves outside their own premises, for example
the . . . school has a small reserve . . .
of about half an acre with a spring and wood. In all these cases we get the school to set up a Reserve Committee on the same lines as County Trust Reserves. The Conservation Officer will be an *ex officio* member and we want to get children involved in the control of the reserves and to draw up management plans. At present we have about one dozen reserves in the county.

Many of the features which follow would find a place in a reserve such as this but they are listed under separate headings because not all schools have areas for reserves. Nevertheless they can attract wildlife to the site with such a feature as a flower border in front of the school which might play its part in attracting butterflies.

An interesting approach to the design of a wildlife area was put forward by the Northumberland and Durham Naturalists Trust and the Hancock Museum in connection with a competition for primary schools called *Rescue* (1969) which they organised for European Conservation Year. Children were asked to discover all they could about animals, birds, insects and so on and then to plan a small hypothetical 'garden' to accommodate them:

Our towns and villages get bigger and spread out into the countryside which gets smaller. If this goes on there will not be much countryside left. And that would make our weekend trips pretty uninteresting wouldn't it? Can we do anything? Yes, of course, we can. Round lots of our houses and schools and other buildings are

GARDENS. This is a competition to work out how we can best make a garden like a bit of real countryside. Not all schools have gardens, especially in the middle of towns but never mind, imagine one, about the size of a tennis court. Learn all you can about wildlife, animals, birds, insects and so on, work out what kind of countryside they like and plan a bit. Draw a plan, paint pictures and make models, your teacher will explain more about it.

Nature trails in the Outside Resource Area

Since their first use in Britain in the early 1960s, nature trails have been popular among teachers for introducing field study activities. They found the programmed route, with its guidebook information pinpointing major matters of interest, an attractive and time-saving way of conducting a field trip. At first they used the trails prepared by a variety of organisations for public use. Then individuals and groups began to prepare trails specifically for their pupils; recently some teachers have looked upon them as incentives for firsthand enquiry methods and have set their children to making their own trails.

Most prepared trails are some distance from the school, so using them has meant a journey from school, often rearrangement of the timetable and sometimes difficulties with staffing the visit adequately. Subsequent visits to follow up particular things in which pupils have shown special interest are difficult in those circumstances. Some trails have been so overused by school parties that visits have to be restricted and there is a waiting list.

Some teachers have developed successful nature trails in their school grounds, sometimes providing a complete route for the children to follow, while in other cases the site has been used for groups of children to make their own trails. Apart from the obvious ease of access and the lack of travel organisation needed, there are several distinct advantages to be gained from using the school grounds.

Because the school has control over design and management it is possible to introduce features which meet the specific needs of the children involved. The facilities which a trail elsewhere offers may not fulfil the needs of your course.

Follow-up visits are no problem. Children can pursue points of interest at any time, in succeeding lessons or in their own time, without the teacher having to make special plans. Where the trail is used to stimulate enquiry methods (that is where pupils make their own trail, investigating the site and finding out more about the interesting things discovered) frequent visits to areas of activity are necessary and the use of school grounds obviously makes this easier.

Inside the school boundary, the teacher's task of overseeing is much easier and his responsibilities are less than if pupils have to leave the premises.

In Project Environment's investigations into the use of trails as an aid to teaching, several schools developed trails in their grounds. They showed that even grounds not specifically designed as an educational resource can be used successfully. Where estates are planned as outdoor resource areas the possibilities are very much greater. The full account of the use of trails as an educational resource and the references to school estates for this purpose are in Project Environment's *Learning from Trails* (Longman 1974).

Encouraging a rich variety of living things

Plant life

Trees and shrubs

One of the richest resources on the school estate is undoubtedly provided by trees and shrubs. Their variety of form and habit, the range of habitats they create and the other organisms which become associated with them and the opportunities they provide for realistic studies in most subject areas, from the mathematical to the artistic, make them essential to any school site where they will grow.
Some of the criteria for choosing trees might be:

Biological interest
Tree studies are well established in schools so there is no need to list the features which might be studied. The important thing here is that variety is needed—broadleaf trees, conifers, evergreen, deciduous, large and small and so on.

General educational interest

The variety essential for satisfying biological interest provides a wealth of material for other subject studies. Many schools already use trees and shrubs as a stimulus for creative writing of poetry and prose, as a source of art inspiration, as the basis of some aspects of history and geography studies and for simple arithmetical and geometrical work. Some of this work is described in such publications as the Schools Council Science 5/13 Project, *Trees Stage 1 and 2* (Macdonald Educational, 1973), and the Forestry Commission booklet, *Forestry and the Town School* by D. Healey (1967).

Beauty

If we are to make children environmentally aware, we ought to see that the school environment is as pleasant as possible and that the children are conscious of the factors involved. The school ought also to be an example to the local community. Probably no single feature would do more to settle the school in the landscape and relieve the hardness of its appearance than groups of large established trees. Unfortunately this takes time, but somebody must make a start. We would not enjoy the beauty of trees now if our forebears had not planted them for the future.

Some trees grow very fast, and backed by similarly fast-growing shrubs they can transform a site, give shelter and add their unique beauty in a remarkably short time. Present attempts at this are usually limited to ornamental planting round the buildings. Little is done to try to make the site as a whole an attractive place, yet the cost of this would be quite trivial in the total cost of the school. Often the money provided for site planting in a new school would be adequate if it were used more effectively. A sum that will provide a few trees and shrub borders round the buildings can provide the money for more extensive plantings if it is spent on trees to be planted by the children. The more they can be involved, not merely in the planting, but in the planning of development and management, the more the trees and the site as a whole will mean to them. Where adequate consultation is possible between architects, ground maintenance staff, advisers and school staff this way of working has proved very successful.

The beauty of the individual tree or shrub near the buildings can be studied and appreciated at a more intimate level. Here one is not thinking primarily of the mock oranges and other common subjects

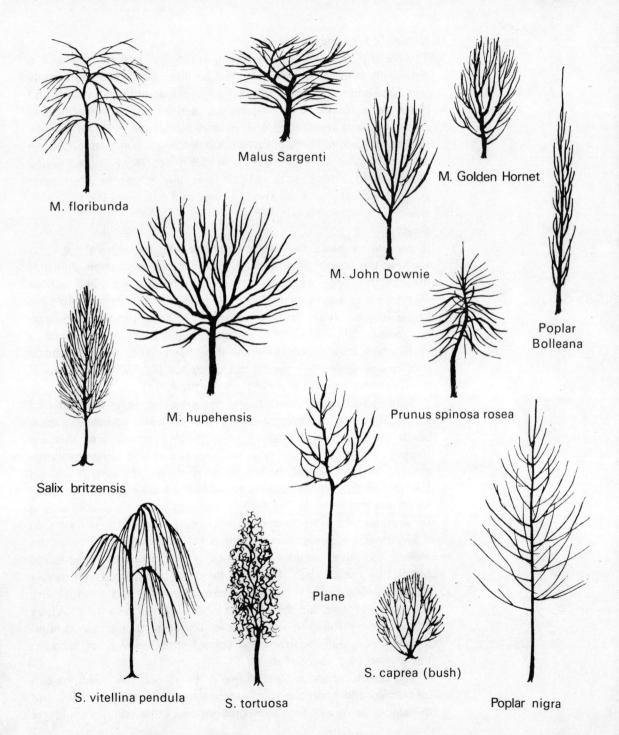

M. floribunda

Malus Sargenti

M. Golden Hornet

M. John Downie

Poplar
Bolleana

Salix britzensis

M. hupehensis

Prunus spinosa rosea

S. vitellina pendula

S. tortuosa

Plane

S. caprea (bush)

Poplar nigra

that fill many shrub borders but trees and shrubs grown specifically for variety of form, for example fastigiate, weeping, rounded, spreading and so on; for beauty of foliage, such as coloured, variegated, shining, dissected, autumn colour; for attractiveness of bark, for example orange, yellow, blue in willows, red in dogwood, white in birches, striped in maples, polished in cherries and maples; and for a variety of other qualities.

Even within a single species it is possible to show great variety in appearance. The forms of common beech illustrate the range available within a single species. There are normal, weeping and fastigate growth habits, normal and fern leaved forms and copper, purple, yellow and variegated foliage species. The mountain ashes also show great variety of fruit colour, autumn colouring, foliage characteristics and growth habits.

Value in encouraging wildlife
Lists under 'Bird life' (p. 79) and 'Insect life (p. 83–9) give some indication of the value of various trees and shrubs for this purpose.

Value as illustrations of important crop plants
Timber, paper and the forest products are of enormous importance in our everyday lives and even in a country as little forested as ours, timber is still an important crop. Great Britain has 1 200 000 hectares of forest trees, compared with 800 000 hectares of wheat. The Forestry Commission *Census of Woodland 1965/67* (HMSO) shows the relative importance of various forest trees in England, to be as follows (figures in thousand hectares):

Broadleaved		Conifers	
	thousand hectares		thousand hectares
oak	141	Scots pine	98
beech	53	Sitka spruce	49
ash	27	Norway spruce	41
sycamore	20	European larch	34
poplar	7	Japanese and hybrid larch	31
birch	7	Corsican pine	30
elm	7	Douglas fir	24
chestnut	4½	lodgepole pine	9
		western hemlock	3
		western red cedar	2
◀ branching of some trees		others	11

In addition there were under coppice:

	thousand hectares
hazel	3
hornbeam	6

It would seem that all these species are important enough to be planted in a representative school forestry collection.

Occasions will no doubt arise when children want to be able to discover which timber comes from which tree, but timber names do not always tally with those of the trees which produce them.
For example:

Lebanon cedar, mentioned in the Bible, is the wood of *Cedrus libani,* a true cedar.

White cedar is from *Thuja occidentalis.* Western red cedar is from *Thuja plicata.*

Virginian pencil cedar is from *Juniperus virginiana,* a juniper.

Port Orford cedar is from Lawson's cypress, *Chamaecyparis lawsoniana.*

Oregon pine is from the Douglas fir, *Pseudotsuga douglasii.*

Redwood, also known as 'red deal', is from Scots pine, *Pinus sylvestris.*

Whitewood, or 'white deal' is from the Norway spruce, *Picea abies.*

Yellow deal, also known as 'yellow pine' is from the maritime pine, *Pinus strobus.*

In addition to the usual forestry species a collection of trees and shrubs grown for past and present uses of their timber might include:

alder	turnery, clogs, charcoal
alder, buckthorn	charcoal for gunpowder
ash, coppiced	garden tool handles, hockey sticks
box	rulers, fine turnery and carving
chestnut (sweet) coppiced	fencing
dogwood	skewers
gean (wild cherry)	turnery, veneers
hazel	wattle
holly	turnery, inlaying, carving
hornbeam	mallets, turnery, yokes
lime	carving
maple, field	fine turnery
maple, Norway	veneers, flooring
pear	carving, engraving
spindle	artist's charcoal
tulip tree	canary wood for fine joinery

| walnut | veneers |
| willow | *Salix alba* var. *coerulea* is the cricket bat willow; *Salix viminalis* is the osier used for basketry |

Speed of growth

Fast growth is desirable, but many of the most interesting and important species, such as our native oak, are slow growing. However, slow growers are usually shade tolerant so they can be planted amongst groups of faster-growing trees which they will eventually overtake. Children are understandably impatient to see results so a backbone of rapidly growing trees and shrubs is very desirable. Poplars are very fast growing (it is well to remember that not all poplars are shaped like the Lombardy poplar, *Populus italica*).

A Forestry Commission trial gave the following average heights of some poplars at eighteen years:

P. androscoggin	28.3 m
P. trichocarpa	28.7 m
P. robusta (trial 1)	26.2 m
P. robusta (trial 2)	24.7 m

Willows too are very fast growing and can be cut back every year or two to promote a dense screen.

Cotoneaster frigida and the variety *Cornubia* are amongst the fastest growing evergreen or semi-evergreen plants in the country. They will grow 4.5 m high and as wide in a few years.

Of the conifers *Cupressocyparis leylandii* (often called *Cupressus leylandii*) is the fastest. It is still relatively uncommon and expensive, however, but it is fairly easy to propagate from cuttings.

Fast-growing	**slow growing**
ash	beech
larch	oak
Cupressocyparis leylandii	yew
poplar (particularly balsam poplars and their hybrids)	cedar
sycamore	
birch	
alder	
bird cherry	
willow	
elder	
Cotoneaster frigida var. *Cornubia*	

It is impossible to categorise too precisely in this respect, however, for conditions of soil and site have a tremendous effect. Even on the same site Forestry Commission trials show great differences in trees planted in successive years.

Undesirable features

Conker trees always seem to attract a hail of brickbats from small boys. There are non-fruiting varieties which may be used where this is a problem. Apples and blackberries might also attract unwanted visitors.

Trees with large leaves such as sycamore and horse chestnut are unpopular because their fallen leaves are a nuisance, and some say a danger, because of their slipperiness.

Poplars have a reputation for doing damage to drains and foundations when planted close to buildings and when used for quick cover should be felled as soon as others have developed. Ash, elm and willow are also suspect. Some varieties of poplar are very susceptible to canker and these should be avoided.

Trees which have dense foliage should not be planted close enough to buildings to create unwanted shade. The silver birch is ideal in this situation for its year-round beauty and the very light shade it casts. Elm has a reputation for shedding branches. In any case incidence of Dutch elm disease makes it wise to avoid planting this tree.

Lime though popular with beekeepers is unpopular where cars are parked because of the honeydew which its insect population showers down on the vehicles.

Obtaining trees and planting them

Obtaining trees, planting them and maintaining them appears to present problems to some schools who wish to do their own planting.

The following advice taken from the Forestry Commission leaflet *Starting a School Forest* (1968) may be of help.

Gifts of trees for planting in school precincts

. . . the Forestry Commission will consider making gifts of up to 100 young forest trees for planting for study purposes in school grounds or playing fields, or of smaller numbers for raising in pots

tree planting in school grounds

in the classroom. The offer is conditional on the Commission having a surplus of such trees and on the school being prepared to meet the cost (which would be small) of packing and transport. Application should be made to the appropriate Conservator during the summer preceding each autumn-spring planting season, to give him time to reserve stocks . . .

Planting of trees in school grounds

The principal trees now being planted in British forests are as follows: conifers: Scots pine; Corsican pine; lodgepole pine; European larch; Japanese larch; Douglas fir; Norway spruce; sitka spruce: hardwoods: beech; oak; sycamore; birch; ash.

The following notes apply to softwoods and hardwoods planted under conditions likely to be met in school grounds or playing fields, and similar sites. Trees should be planted as soon as possible after receipt, but they will take no harm for a few days provided their roots are kept constantly moist. The best way to do this is to heel the trees in, by setting their roots in a shallow trench and covering them over with damp earth.

When to plant

Planting should only be done during the 'resting' season of the tree, which extends from October to the end of April. No attempt should be made to plant trees when the ground is frost-bound, and it is preferable that planting should take place when the soil is moist.

Choice of site

Any reasonably fertile and well-drained soil is suitable for the growth of the aforementioned forest trees. In windswept areas, they will benefit greatly by shelter from a hedge or wall. It must be borne in mind that, although the trees are quite small when planted they may eventually grow to heights between 15 and 30 metres, or even more. In siting them in school precincts, or around playing fields, one must keep in mind their eventual height and the spread of their roots and crowns, which may be considerable. They should not be put too close to buildings or in situations where they might obstruct overhead wires, or the light reaching windows.

Spacing

Where the object is to form a small wood or shelterbelt, the trees should be set about 1.5 metres apart each way. Later on, perhaps after ten or fifteen years, when they have grown much larger, some can be thinned out to give the others more room, and the timber put to some useful purpose.

Where single specimen trees are planted, at least 3 metres should be left between each of them.

Ground preparation and planting

It is advisable to use the pit method of planting, although in forestry practice, where much larger numbers of trees have to be dealt with, the simpler and cheaper notch method is more usual.

When pit planting, the soil should be dug with a garden fork or spade to a depth of about 30 cm., and thoroughly broken up. As much of this cultivated soil as necessary should be taken out of the hole. Then the young tree should be inserted in it, with its roots disposed as naturally as possible, and held *at exactly the same depth as it grew in the nursery*, while the excavated soil is returned. The right depth can be found by looking closely for the collar of the tree—that is the point where the underground roots and the shoot join.

It is important to make the soil really firm around the roots, by pressing it down with the foot. Watering should not be necessary, except in very dry weather.

Weeding, staking and protection

If, in succeeding summers, grass or weeds grow over the planting site, it should be trimmed back, and the cuttings spread as a mulch around the stems of the young trees. This work may have to be done for two or three years before the trees have grown tall enough to be quite safe from becoming overgrown or suppressed.

As a rule, no staking will be needed, but if it is desired to support a young stem, it may be fastened to a suitable stake, driven firmly into the ground a few centimetres from the tree, with a band of sacking or similar soft material; wire should never be used.

Young trees must be protected, *at all times*, from damage by grazing livestock or rabbits. It is useless to plant them where there is any risk from these animals. As a rule, the existing fences will be adequate to safeguard them from domestic animals but where *any* rabbits are found, wire netting of 3 cm mesh, and one metre high, with a further 15 cm buried below ground (or bent outwards at ground level and held down by stones or clods), is essential for protection. This can be set up with the aid of a stake as a sleeve around individual trees or attached to an ordinary post and wire fence around a group.

Planting in pots
Where no outdoor planting sites are available, the young trees may be grown for several years in pots, indoors or out, provided they are given ample daylight and regularly watered.

It has to be pointed out that the trees supplied are very small, usually no more than 30 cm high.

Where larger standard trees are planted, 2.5–3 metres high, careful staking with stout 5–8 cm diameter posts is needed. These must be driven firmly into the ground before the tree is planted. The trees should be secured to the stake with a tie that has a protective pad of some kind between stake and tree to prevent damage to the bark from rubbing. Stakes are usually put on the side of the tree facing the prevailing wind but with trees planted along the edges of mown areas it may be a wise precaution to put the stake towards the mown area so that carelessly-manoeuvred gang mowers hit the stake and not the tree.

The tree nursery
A few square metres of ground on which trees can be raised adds greatly to the educational scope of tree studies as well as having the practical advantage of providing a supply of trees for planting in and beyond the school grounds.

Children may be able to collect some seed locally, particularly of oak, beech, ash, sycamore and birch. Conifer seed may have to be purchased. One firm which deals in tree seed is Benjamin Reid & Co. Ltd, Pinewood Park Nurseries, Countesswells Road, Aberdeen. Another which also supplies seedlings is English Woodlands Ltd, The Old Malt House, 125 High Street, Uckfield, Sussex.

A Dunemann seedbed gives a reliable way of raising tree seedlings if it is sited out of doors in a position protected from wind. A wooden frame, say 1.25 m × 1 m and 30 cm high, would be a suitable container to start with. Put a few centimetres of cinders or ash in the bottom for drainage. Then fill the box with needle litter from the floor of a pinewood; leaf mould or even a mixture of peat and sand will do if pine litter is not available. The top should be firm and level and the seeds can be sown in shallow drills, being covered with litter to about twice their thickness. It will be necessary to cover the top with fine mesh wire netting to keep birds and mice away.

Poplars and willows are ideal subjects for propagation in school since they root easily (from hardwood cuttings about 25 cm long and 1 to 2 cm thick) and their very fast growth is exciting to children: Two metres of growth from a poplar cutting in the first season is worth watching!

In order to get quick results, the temptation is to plant large trees but in the school situation it is often better to plant a cluster of small trees instead of one bigger specimen. They usually grow faster and catch up after a few years and can be thinned out as necessary. Should losses occur, from whatever cause, there is a better chance of there being some survivors than when all the eggs are in one basket.

Tree planting schemes
If a surplus of young trees is raised there is the possibility of carrying out some sort of tree planting scheme outside the school. Local civic and amenity trusts will often help here. The opportunity for pupils to raise trees in school and then prepare planting and management schemes jointly with trust officers can lead to a useful drawing together of school and the local community. The most important aspect of this is the reality of the school's work in the eyes of the pupils and their direct participation in the affairs of *their* community.

Plant collections

There is an almost endless number of ways in which plants could be grouped so as to bring together collections of plants to illustrate habit of growth, characters of leaf, stem, flowers, etc., methods of pollination, seed dispersal and vegetative spread, historical, geographical and other associations, past and present uses and so on. The following suggestions are no more than an indication of some possibilities for sets of plants that could be grown for comparative studies and other purposes.

Growth habit

Many plants have similar habits but use varied ways of expressing them. For example, a group of plants could be arranged to illustrate methods of climbing. Some structure would be needed for them to climb on, either living or dead plants or a specially constructed framework. Thin canes, twiggy branches and thicker poles could be added to provide for all climbing methods. Plants which could be used include:

scramblers	rose, bramble, hedge bedstraw *(Gallium mollugo)* and cleavers or goosegrass, *(Gallium aparine)*
root climbers	ivy
tendril climbers	clematis and nasturtium (sensitive petioles) peas, vetches (leaf tendrils), *(Bryonia dioica),* marrows (stem tendrils)
twiners	honeysuckle, runner beans, hop, black bryony *(Tamus communis)*

Stem structure

Non-climbing plants use their stems alone to support them and stem structures vary in many ingenious ways to provide strong support for a minimum of material. Suitable plants include:

tubular stems	wheat, dandelion
hollow stems with buttressing	cow parsley, celery, parsley, mint, deadnettle
pith-filled stems	hollyhock, sedge *(Scirpus)*, elder
woody stems	willow or any other woody perennial

Variety of form within a family

Many plant families have great variety of form although floral parts are similar. A group of *Papillionaceae* to show this might include:

tree forms	the locust tree *(Robinia)*, Judas tree *(Cercis)*
shrub forms	gorse, broom, bladder senna *(Colutia)*
herbaceous forms erect	broad bean, French bean, lupin, sweet clover
climbing	runner bean, garden pea, sweet pea, vetches
creeping	white clover, yellow medick

Enthusiastic botanists may wish to carry this idea further to provide a wide range of plant life-forms.

Seed dispersal methods

A bed of plants selected to illustrate the variety of seed dispersal would be a source of interest and could include maple for its winged seeds, clematis for its feathered seeds, poppy for its censer action, goosegrass and burdock for their hooked fruits, geranium, gorse and balsam for their explosive mechanisms and fleshy fruiting plants such as raspberries. Such a seed dispersal set could be coupled with a dispersal plot, for example a plot cleared of vegetation with, say a balsam plant set in the middle so that the appearance of seedlings around it could be plotted to indicate the spread of its seed dispersal mechanism.

A comparable collection could be used to illustrate vegetative spread of cultivated and wild plants, especially weeds. In like manner a plot could be set aside to show the rate of spread of a plant such as strawberry, creeping red fescue or couch grass.

In America a strong line stretched between posts over cultivated soil so as to form a perch for birds is sometimes used to give a plow perch planting. Shrub seedlings growing up from bird droppings provide a natural hedge if the birds can be induced to perch on the line.

Dyestuffs

The preparation and use of vegetable dyes fascinates children. The following list, adapted from Violetta Thurstan's *The Use of Vegetable Dyes* (Dryad Press), gives some plants found in this country which may be used for this purpose.

In addition the following make good dyes and could be grown in the garden: onion (skins), beetroot, red cabbage, woad.

Indicators. A number of plants contain colours which change according to the acidity or alkalinity of the surrounding liquid and therefore act as indicators. Litmus, obtained from lichens, is one of these. Most strongly coloured purple fruits give colours which act in this way, for example blackberry, damson, elderberry, bilberry. Red cabbage juice is yellow when very alkaline, green when moderately alkaline, purplish when neutral and reddish in acid solution (as when pickled in vinegar) and is a good indicator.

yellow	green	brown	black	red	blue	orange	purple
alder	alder	blackberry	blackberry	bedstraw	bearberry	weld	birch bark
apple	bearberry	juniper	elder	*(Galium	blackberry	*(Reseda*	damson
ash	bracken	larch	meadow-	boreale)*	cornflower	*luteola)*	
barberry	elder	oak	sweet	blackberry	dog's mercury		
bedstraw	horsetail	pine cones	walnut	iris	devil's bit		
(Galium	ling	sloe		*(I. pseuda-*	scabious		
boreale)	privet	walnut		*corus)*	sloe		
birch bark	reeds						
bracken	tansy						
broom	tamarisk						
camomile							
(Anthemis							
tinctoria)							
dog's mercury							
dyer's							
greenweed							
golden rod							
gorse							
ling							
marsh							
marigold							
pear							
pine cones							
privet							
plum leaves							
poplar leaves							
ragwort							
tansy							
weld							
(Reseda							
luteola)							

Other collections
Other plant groupings that have proved successful in schools include:

geographical	plants from various countries or continents planted together
historical	plants with historical association such as the York and Lancaster rose and woad. Also plants grouped according to the time of introduction to this country—those introduced by the Romans, the Crusaders, following early exploration of America, by plant hunters in the Himalayas and south-west China and so on
biblical	association such as St John's wort, blessed thistle and Lady's mantle
pollination	interesting pollination mechanisms such as sage, *Mimulus, Lythrum* and primrose.

A whole range of groupings is possible to illustrate botanical and horticultural features such as: autumn colour, coloured bark, foliage colour, variation within a species, hybrids with their parents, parasites and hosts and non-flowering plants.

Food plants could be grouped under such headings as:

seeds we eat	peas, broad beans, wheat (though technically a fruit!)
fruits we eat	tomato, marrow
leaves we eat	spinach, lettuce
stems we eat	asparagus, rhubarb, potato
buds we eat	cauliflower, globe artichoke, Brussels sprouts
roots we eat	carrot, parsnip

R. H. Thomas in an article on 'The botanic garden in geography teaching' in the *Journal of the Geographical Association* (November 1971) says:

A list of plant groups to look for during fieldwork at a botanic garden might therefore include:
plants with features showing adaptation to a foreign climatic environment,
plants with fruit or seeds which are of economic importance,
staple food crops from various parts of the world,
plants whose leaves, stems and trunks are used by man,
plants whose 'natural' distribution has been extended through cultivation by man in a botanic garden,
plants with unusual growing habits.

While this refers to public gardens, the school grounds could provide this sort of material.

Wildflowers and weeds

A varied ground flora will be an asset in any area devoted to the protection and study of wildlife. The smaller plants will provide food for insects and other small creatures, cover for small mammals, reptiles and amphibia and food for some birds. They will of course be needed for study on their own account. There is not likely to be any difficulty in getting a good ground cover of common weeds, even in towns. What will probably be lacking is the variety of plants that would seem desirable and it may be necessary to add to the range of species available or to fill some specific need.

Great care should be taken not to harm wild plant communities when building up such collections. The following is an extract from the Botanical Society of the British Isles' *Code of Conduct for the conservation of wild plants:*

Collecting

7 The uprooting of wild plants is to be strongly discouraged, except, with discrimination, weeds. Most local authorities have bye-laws against this, so it may well be illegal.

8 If living plants are needed for cultivation, take seed or cuttings sparingly, and not from those that are rare.

9 Pick only flowers known to be common or plentiful in the locality but whenever you can, leave them for others to enjoy. If you wish to identify a plant, take the smallest adequate bit; often a photograph may serve the purpose.

10 No specimens should be taken from any nature reserve, nature trail, National Trust property or a designated Site of Special Scientific Interest.

11 In particular teachers, organisers of wild flower competitions and leaders of outings and field meetings should bear these points in mind.

(The *Code* is obtainable from the BSBI, c/o The Department of Botany, British Museum (Natural History), Cromwell Road, London SW7.)

Surface soil usually contains large numbers of seeds from surrounding vegetation and soil collected and spread out to allow these to germinate may yield a useful crop of wild plants.

Weed study

A common definition of a weed is a plant growing where it is not wanted. While this is true, it does not make plain two characteristics of familiar weeds which make them such a nuisance in farm, forest and garden—that is persistence (the ability of the species to maintain itself over a long period) and aggressiveness (the tendency to spread). It is these two characteristics which make weeds such a nuisance in gardens and farms. They are amongst the most important plants we have, yet they are strangely neglected in our studies. Weeds in the school grounds and particularly on the cultivated plots are usually regarded as a nuisance to be destroyed as quickly as possible, yet there are good reasons for studying them. In particular, the way they achieve persistence and aggressiveness can give rise to useful practical ecological work.

Among other reasons for making provision for the study of weeds are:

They are of enormous importance. World crop losses due to weeds are estimated at about £8 000 million, about 15% of the total crop values. This is comparable to the losses due to pests and to diseases. They are easily available! They are plentiful, grow anywhere, cost nothing and are available for study at all seasons. They are quick and easy to grow.

They can be collected freely. Their use could relieve pressure on fieldwork resources outside the school.

There are a limited number of species, mostly familiar, so that identification is not the bugbear that it can be when studying wild plant communities. There is abundant information about them and identification guides are available for all stages, for example seed, seedlings and mature plants. Nevertheless, they offer plenty of variety of form and ecology.

They are a wild population yet they have a direct influence on man as he has on them.

To facilitate these studies the following provisions might be made.

Wasteland

If there are any rough, weedy, neglected areas on the site, as may be the case with new schools, a small area should be retained so that the coarse weeds of waste ground—docks, nettles, thistles, bindweed, etc., can be allowed to flourish (see note about 'Weeds and neighbours' on p. 70).

Grassland

Areas of grass should be set aside, some on fine turf and others on coarser grassland of playing fields. On these the effects on weed population of such factors as mowing, wear and fertiliser treatment can be studied. A good deal of work can be carried out on lawns,

cricket squares and sports pitches without interfering in any way
with their normal use and maintenance, but small areas which can
be treated differently are also desirable.

Arable
Small cultivated areas for the study of arable weeds are useful.
Again, a good deal can be done on plots used for growing plants
for other purposes but for some work it is desirable to have small
areas set aside specifically for weed study. For example, succession
plots show how species supersede each other.

Succession plots
If a bare piece of ground is left, what are the stages of colonisation?
One could have a miniature version of the famous one at Rothamsted
Broadbalk Field in which an area was left entirely alone and other
parts were cultivated at different intervals to enable comparisons of
the stages of plant succession to be made. Similar arrangements
could be made on grassland and wasteland areas.

   The areas required for these purposes depend to a large extent
on the amount of use they will receive. Obviously, if a number of
classes are going to use any area regularly, then it may suffer from
excessive wear and tear if it is not of adequate size. Another consideration is edge effect. If it is desired to study a square metre
of cultivated land, a plot of just that size cut out of turf will be
unsatisfactory for the edges of the plot will be affected by the different
conditions in the turf. A plot of say 2 by 2 metres would be needed
so that the sample area could be sited clear of the turf.

Weeds and neighbours
Weedy patches in school are liable to upset the neighbours and
administrators who do not understand what they are there for and
who may think of them as signs of untidiness and neglect. Clear and
tidy outlines of these areas and bold labelling can help to correct this
impression. So can careful siting so that they are screened from
obvious view. The weeds must not constitute an actual nuisance by
being allowed to seed into neighbours' gardens and there may be
some conflict between the school's needs and the interests of good
public relations here. According to the law the owner or occupier
of land may be required to prevent the spread of scheduled weeds.
At present these are:

spear thistle	*(Cirsium vulgare)*
field thistle	*(Cirsium arvensis)*
curled dock	*(Rumex crispus)*
broad leaved dock	*(Rumex obtusifolius)*
ragwort	*(Senecio jacobaea)*

However, careful management by the timely removal of all seed heads except sufficient for study purposes (and control of seed dispersal of these) may avoid conflict and conform with the law.

The artificial creation of plant communities

Physical factors play a major part in determining the nature of plant communities. In turn the nature of animal communities is generally determined by the plant community. Much of the character of the living world developed in the school estate will be determined by such things as soil, temperature ranges, rainfall, humidity levels and duration and intensity of sunlight. While our climate permits a wide range of plants and animals to thrive, we can do little to extend that range unless we use a glasshouse, which is really a controlled environment chamber. However, we can extend the range out of doors to some extent by manipulating soil type and conditions. Thus, if we accept the climatic limitations but provide special soil conditions, it is possible to introduce plants which grow within those climatic limitations but which will not normally thrive in the locality due to their different soil needs. In a few cases physical changes in the soil can have some localised effects on the micro-climate, so extending the richness of life on the estate a little further.

Lime-loving plants
At its simplest a small area of well-limed, well drained soil with a pH of about eight will suffice for many of these plants. However, if some limestone can be bought, a raised bed surrounded by a 0.75 m to 1 m dry limestone wall filled with a mixture of non-acid soil and limestone chippings makes a more attractive and obviously limestone habitat.

Many gardening books list calciphilous plants which could be planted on the limestone garden but a limestone/chalk pasture of the grasses *Festuca ovina*, *Agrostis vulgaris*, *Cynosurus cristatus* and *Briza media* could form a basis with such plants as horse-shoe vetch (*Hippocrepis comosa*), clustered bell flower (*Campanula glomerata*), pasque flower (*Anemone pulsatilla*) and wild mignonette (*Reseda lutea*) planted between. If the bed is large enough for shrubs, yew (*Taxus baccata compacta*) is a slow-growing dwarf species, clematis (*Clematis vitalba*), the old man's beard of lime-stone country, or *Viburnum lantana*, are typical calciphilous shrubby plants.

A larger habitat in the form of a chalk mound suitable for schools which have access to two lorry loads of chalk, is described by J. C. Doyle in an article on 'A chalk mound nature reserve', in the *Journal of the National Rural and Environmental Studies Association*, 1970. The chalk is piled over a central core of brick rubble, the topmost layer being crushed to form a seed bed in which *Festuca ovina* and *Festuca rubra* are sown to bind the surface. Doyle suggests constructing passages from the exterior to the core of the mound for introduced common lizards. He recommends seed sowing of plants and has had success with the following:

cowslip	(*Primula veris*)
common rockrose	(*Helianthemum nummularium*)
restharrow	(*Ononis repens*)
birds' foot trefoil	(*Lotus corniculatus*)
horseshoe vetch	(*Hippocrepis comosa*)
salad burnet	(*Sanguisorba minor*)
creeping cinquefoil	(*Potentilla reptans*)
small scabious	(*Scabiosa columbaria*)
field scabious	(*Knautia arvensis*)
ground thistle	(*Cirsium acaule*)
mouse-ear chickweed	(*Hieracium pilosella*)
eyebright	(*Euphrasia nemorosa*)
hayrattle	(*Rhinanthus minor*)
marjoram	(*Origanum vulgare*)
thyme	(*Thymus pulegiodes*)
hoary plantain	(*Plantago media*)
glaucous sedge	(*Carex flacca*)
quaking grass	(*Briza media*)

A heathland plant community
For this it is necessary to produce an area of well drained, sandy soil with peat. The problem on school estates with calcareous soils is to prevent calcium leaching into an artificial calcifuge habitat and a raised bed of peat and calcium-free sand mixture held in place by peat block walls is the best way to construct such a

feature. Make a grass heath by planting *Aira flexuosa, Anthoxanthum odoratum* interplanted with heather (*Calluna vulgaris*), bilberry (*Vaccinium myrtillus*), tormentil (*Potentilla erecta*), gorse (*Ulex europaeus*). Never water the bed with tap water containing lime. An annual treatment with chelated iron (essential iron and other elements in a form which remains available to plants) will help to correct the effects of any spread of calcium from surrounding soil.

A moorland plant community

In general these habitats are wet to waterlogged. A similar bed to that for heathland, supported by peat blocks but composed mostly of peat with only a little lime-free sand will suffice. Mat grass (*Nardus stricta*) will thrive if the peat is not too wet and purple moorgrass (*Molinia caerulea*) if the drainage is poor, as will cross-leaved heath (*Erica tetralix*), toad rush (*Juncus bufonius*) and cotton grass (*Eriophorum vaginatum*). Keep well watered with lime-free water.

Marsh plant communities

A marsh habitat is best built adjacent to a pond so that the plastic liner can be extended from the pond under the soil to provide a waterproof lining 30–60 cm below the marsh and bog, backfilling the marsh area with soil. A true marsh has an average water level which is just under the soil. Typical marsh plants are:

marsh marigold	(*Caltha palustris*)
marsh violet	(*Viola palustris*)
marsh stitchwort	(*Stellaria uliginosa*)
marsh club rush	(*Scirpus palustris*)
marsh penny wort	(*Hydrocotyle vulgaris*)
bog pimpernel	(*Anagallis tenella*)
grass of parnassus	(*Parnassia palustris*)

Wall plant community

Walls provide a dry substrate, poor in nutrients, but even brick walls develop plant communities. A stone wall with the stones held together with mud instead of mortar will more quickly produce a community. Useful plants for setting as seeds in the spaces between stones include:

stonecrop	*(Sedum acre)*
pearlwort	*(Sagina procumbens)*
rue-leafed saxifrage	*(Saxifraga tridactylites)*
ivy-leaved toadflax	*(Linaria cymbalaria)*
house leek	*(Sempervivum tectorum)*
pellitory-of-the-wall	*(Parietaria officinalis)*
pennywort	*(Cotyledon umbilicus)*
wallflower	*(Cheiranthus cheiri)*

Ferns include:

Asplenium ruta muraria
Polypodium vulgare
Adiantum capillus-veneris
Asplenium lanceolatum

Woodland plant communities

Where a soil type has been created by one of the methods described above, or more particularly where there is a chance to diversify the interest of a piece of unused ground, the opportunity exists to plant the native trees which would occur naturally in such a situation. By careful selection of appropriate species of trees and the inclusion of some of the associated understorey shrubs and ground flora to form undergrowth, it is possible to create small woodland ecosystems within school grounds, demonstrating the species composition and structure of woodland communities. The trees should be planted close enough together to constitute a distinct group, but allowing enough space for the canopies to enlarge as the trees mature.

Natural regeneration may occur and should be allowed to develop as this is the way in which woods replenish themselves and saplings contribute to the diversity of structure. Similarly trees which fall or have to be felled should be left in situ as dead timber is an integral part of the woodland ecosystem and the invertebrates and fungi which recycle the constituents into the soil make an interesting study in themselves.

The type of woodland which can be created depends on the soil and water conditions which are available or can be created. The following table indicates associations of trees, shrubs, and ground flora suitable for various soil conditions; representing woodland communities native to the British Isles.

	Trees	**Shrubs**	**Ground flora**
Oakwood pedunculate oak (fertile soils including clays)	pedunculate oak, ash	hazel holly	bramble, woodsorrel, lesser celandine, wood anemone, bluebell
Sessile oak (lighter, drier more acid soils)	sessile oak, birch, rowan		
Ashwood	ash, yew	hazel, spindle, purging buckthorn	bramble, wood brome-grass, dog's mercury, wild garlic, wild strawberry, ground ivy
Pinewood (sandy, *acid*, heathy soils; peat)	Scots pine, rowan	juniper	heathers *(Calluna, Erica)*, bilberry
Alderwood (wet, humus-rich soil; pond margins)	alder	grey sallow, alder buckthorn	marsh marigold, flag iris, meadow-sweet, sedges, rushes

The diagram on page 50 shows a planting in a secondary school based on these ideas. Plants required approximate heights and costs (1972) were:

		£ p
2 field maple *(Acer campestre)*	1 m	0.10
2 alder *(Alnus glutinosa)*	1 m	0.10
5 ash *(Fraxinus excelsior)*	1 m	0.55
1 rowan *(Sorbus aucuparia)*	1 m	0.22
1 gean *(Prunus avium)*	1 m	0.36
2 bird cherry *(Prunus padus)*	1.5 m	0.84
20 blackthorn *(Prunus spinosa)*	1 m	2.80
20 hazel *(Corylus avellana)*	60 cm	3.60
16 holly *(Ilex aquifolium)*	50 cm	12.48
5 Scots pine *(Pinus sylvestris)*	1 m	0.65
5 guelder rose *(Viburnum opulus)*	1 m	1.50
1 goat willow *(Salix caprea)*	1 m	0.24
3 wych elm *(Ulmus glabra)*	1.5 m	1.92
3 lime *(Tilia cordata)*	1 m	1.02
1 yew *(Taxus baccata)*	1 m	0.72
		£27.10

The following advice was given by the conservation expert who devised the planting plan for the school:

Although the present stocking provides opportunities for field studies, the site could be improved and diversified by the addition of shrubs and trees, suited to the existing woodland.

The planting of trees and shrubs in broad ecological groups could further teaching techniques. While the basic plan may resemble little better than a native arboretum, the naturalising of the shrub layer will, with patience, assume the look of a more balanced woodland. Familiarity with native species should lead to a quicker response by pupils when presented with the identical species but under 'field' conditions.

Planting recommendations

The temptation to plant 'instant' trees, or very large shrubs, should be resisted. Without highly specialised nursery treatment, results can be disappointing, as well as very costly. With too much top growth at the expense of root fibre, the large plants frequently go into check. Should there be a risk of hares and/or rabbits gaining entry into the wood, plastic tree guards will be necessary to prevent ring barking.

Planting should ideally be carried out from November until the end of December. There is still some summer warmth in the ground, and the soil has not yet become completely waterlogged. Plant requirements must be finalised before the end of summer, and orders placed with nurserymen as early as possible, so that stocks can be reserved.

Where funds are limited, planting can be phased over one or more seasons, without detriment to the general scheme. Raising plants by seed or cuttings can form an educational project in itself, to be supplemented by a visit to a commercial tree nursery.

Poisonous plants

The following is a list of plants known to have poisoned humans in this country at one time or another. The victims were usually children, who are attracted to succulent berries. Of course plenty of other plants are poisonous, but they are not usually sufficiently tempting to cause trouble.

It would be very easy to get this matter out of proportion and to scare children into being afraid of plants. After all, privet, potato and rhubarb are all in the list and we could hardly ban these. Risks are relatively small but things do sometimes go wrong with young children. They can be helped to recognise with certainty those wild berries which are good to eat and advised to leave alone anything which they are not sure is safe.

alder buckthorn	hemlock
annual mercury	henbane
autumn crocus *(Colchicum)*	ivy
black bryony	laburnum
black nightshade	monkshood
buckthorn	potato (all except the tubers. Even these contain poison when green)
bulbous-buttercup	*Phytolacca*
columbine	privet
cowbane	rhubarb leaves
cuckoo pint	spindle
Daphne	spurge laurel
deadly nightshade	spurge, particularly caper spurge
dog's mercury	some toadstools
fool's parsley	thorn apple
foxglove	water dropwort
hellebore	woody nightshade

Useful aids to identification are *Poisonous Plants and Fungi in Colour* sponsored by the Pharmaceutical Society (Blandford) and a collection of coloured slides, *Poisonous Plants and Fungi*, with booklet, obtainable only from the Pharmaceutical Press, 17 Bloomsbury Square, London W.C.1. The Ministry of Agriculture Bulletin *British Poisonous Plants* (H.M.S.O.) is also useful.

Non-flowering plants

Horsetails, though frequently plants of wetter places, often occur as weeds of cultivation and it should not prove difficult to collect and introduce them. These are pernicious weeds which are very difficult to eradicate once established so introduction should be made with care and forethought. The stems and leaves of the horsetails are silicaceous. They are reputed to have been used by gypsies as pot scourers.

Mosses occur in a variety of situations and many different substrates—soil, stone, bricks, wood and so on. It should be possible to recreate suitable conditions—usually damp and shady—and introduce them from the wild. *Fontinalis* can be grown in the pond. Some mosses are particularly interesting for their ability to dry out almost completely, for example, those on roofs, and to spring to life again immediately after rain.

Ferns can be raised from spores collected in the wild or bought from seedsmen. Some nurserymen stock them and a few could be collected where they are really abundant. They require shade and wall species could be grown in crevices on the shady side of a wall, while others could be grown in a fern grotto in the shade of trees. The grotto could be simply a steep rockery wall facing north with crevices in which the ferns are planted.

Fungi of the saprophytic fungi type will appear on old tree trunks, posts, bundles of sticks and other dead wood and other organic material. Their action as decomposers can be studied in the changes areas where their usefulness will be particularly apparent in the compost heap. The term non-biodegradable and the problems it connotes may become more realistic here. Organic matter buried under grass may give rise to toadstools while mushrooms can be raised on artificial composts. Where crop plants are grown there will be plenty of parasitic fungi available for study as plant diseases; of course they occur in wild plants as well.

Liverworts can be encouraged by providing damp conditions on suitable substrates—soil, bricks, cinders, etc. They are often a nuisance on pot plants in nurseries and the local nurseryman may be pleased to part with some. They may be established in the fern grotto or in daily watered pots of soil kept in the shade.

Filamentous algae, diatoms and desmids will appear in the pond.

Lichens are a symbiotic relationship of two plants, an alga and a fungus. They occur in many forms and in shady as well as open situations but their presence is restricted by air pollution. The shrubby and leafy lichens, such as hang from trees, are very sensitive to pollution while some of the powdery lichens are much more resistant. In most schools, the provision of stone walling and some wooden fence posts will offer places on which powdery and leafy lichens as well as powdery algae may grow.

Bird life

Bird studies would rank high amongst the uses to which many schools would want to put their outdoor areas. Birds can be encouraged to the school grounds by providing food, water, shelter and nesting sites.

Food

In their leaflet, *Feed the Birds*, the Royal Society for the Protection of Birds (The Lodge, Sandy, Bedfordshire) list the following shrubs as those whose berries are most sought after by birds:

elder (mainly *Sambucus nigra*)
hawthorn (mainly *Crataegus monogyna*)
yew *(Taxus baccata)*
blackberry *(Rubus fruticosus* agg.*)*
Cotoneaster simonsii
Cotoneaster horizontalis
Cotoneaster watereri
rowan *(Sorbus aucuparia)*
barberry *(Berberis darwinii)*
firethorn *(Pyracantha coccinea)*
holly (mainly *Ilex aquifolium*)
crab apple (mainly *Malus pumila*)
flowering currant (mainly *Ribes sanguineum*)
privet (mainly *Ligustrum vulgare*)
spindle tree *(Euonymus europaeus)*
snowberry *(Symphoricarpos rivularis)*
wayfaring tree *(Viburnum lantana)*
honeysuckle *(Lonicera* sp.*)*

and the following plants to provide seeds for birds:

giant sunflower	thistle
Cosmos	knapweed
China aster	teasel
scabious	ragwort
evening primrose	nettle
Antirrhinum	field poppy
Michaelmas daisy	

These could be planted in beds or allowed to grow freely in a wild area. Some birds will feed on the grass areas, some on cultivated ground in the school garden while any steps taken to encourage insects are likely to encourage also some of the birds that feed on them. A pond 3 to 3.5 metres in diameter will often attract enough insects to bring nearby housemartins and swifts.

Bird tables or feeders, with their less natural foods, are probably best set up reasonably close to classroom windows where it is easiest to watch feeding. Situate them close to a few shrubs or small trees in which the birds can perch and 'spy out the land' before visiting the table or feeder perches.

Water

The ponds and pools suggested elsewhere will provide drinking places for birds if they are so arranged that birds can reach the water surface. Where the edge of the pond makes this difficult it may be necessary to provide some small island for this purpose, although in summer the birds will alight on lily and other water plant leaves.

Bird baths

Birds enjoy shallow water in which they can bathe and a shallow bowl on the bird table, a stone sink or a concrete bird bath built as a special feature will attract many of the smaller birds.

Shelter and nest sites

If a good selection of the shrubs and trees listed elsewhere is grown, particularly those of dense growth such as hawthorn, blackberry and holly, birds should have plenty of shelter and sites for nesting. Piles of old brushwood are suggested as an addition by the Royal Society for the Protection of Birds. These can be supplemented by building nest boxes and distributing them on the site, either on trees or on poles.

A universal nesting box for small birds

The illustration shown here is taken from a design supplied to readers of *Wildlife and the Countryside* in the November 1968 issue of the magazine. Experience has shown that it is simple to make and effective as a nesting box. The box is made from a 106 cm ×

making a nesting box

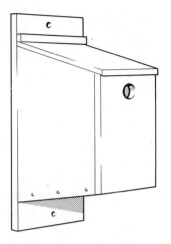

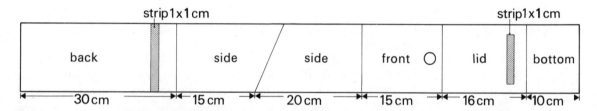

strip 1 x 1 cm   strip 1 x 1 cm

| back | side | side | front ○ | lid | bottom |

30 cm · 15 cm · 20 cm · 15 cm · 16 cm · 10 cm

How to cut your board   13 cm×1 cm board cut as shown in the illustration. Red cedar is a most suitable timber to use because of its resistance to rotting, but white deal which is treated with a preservative is also suitable. Pin the box components together with galvanised panel pins. The lid in this diagram is loose-fitting but secure; the top of the lid fits under the 12 mm×12 mm strip fixed to the back and the lid is prevented from slipping forward by the 12 mm×12 mm strip fixed to its underside.

A hole 30 mm in diameter cut 25 mm below the top will admit blue, coal or great tits, as well as nuthatches and pied flycatchers, but will exclude house sparrows. By cutting off the upper 380 mm of the front to make an open-fronted box you may attract robins, spotted flycatchers, pied wagtails or wrens.

Many other designs for special requirements and for more selective birds, as well as general information on siting, maintaining and methods of recording are described in the British Trust for Ornithology *Field Guide Number Three* (1971) from the B.T.O., Beech Grove, Tring, Hertfordshire.

Observation hides

A small shed, with a board removed at a suitable height so that children can observe while sitting, would make an ideal hide, but is not essential. Children enjoy building their own hide using natural materials.

Alternatively, a cloth hide is easily made using a simple structure of poles or canes covered with canvas or hessian. Take four poles with wood screws or nails protruding 2 cm from one end and stick them, screws uppermost, into the soil. Take four more poles with screw eyes in each end and place the eyes over the screws so that the poles form horizontal crossmembers. Have the canvas sewn up into a suitable shape so that it can be slipped over the pole structure. Leave an entry flap and cut several peep holes so that several people can use the hide at one time.

Insect life

Insects are interesting and often attractive creatures to study, and are usually a good deal easier to observe than wild birds or mammals. A thriving insect population, moreover, is likely to attract these larger wild creatures, so it is worth including plants which encourage and attract them. Judicious collecting is possible so that they can be kept and more closely studied in the classroom, whereas this would not be acceptable with birds and most wild mammals.

Light traps however can collect enormous numbers of insects and may be a serious threat to some local insect populations. Hence it is important to use a trap which does not kill, to empty the traps without undue delay, to retain the minimum number of insects required for study and to release the remainder. The following is an extract from a simplified version of *A Code for Insect Collecting* prepared by the Joint Committee for the Conservation of British Insects:

Collecting-lights and light-traps
The 'catch' at light, particularly in a trap, should not be killed wholesale for subsequent examination.

Live trapping, for instance in traps filled with egg-tray material, is the preferred method of collecting. Anaesthetics are harmful and should not be used.

After examination of the catch the insects should be kept in cool, shady conditions and released away from the trap site at dusk. If this is not possible the insects should be released in long grass or other cover and not on lawns or bare surfaces. Unwanted insects should not be fed to fish or insectivorous birds and mammals.

If a trap used for scientific purposes is found to be catching rare or local species it should be re-sited.

Traps and lights should be sited with care so as not to annoy neighbours or cause confusion.

The following lists show the food plants of our more widespread butterflies and a selection of the larger and commoner moths and some exotic insects:

Food plants of Butterfly and Moth larvae

aspen	poplar kitten, sallow kitten, poplar hawk
beech	sallow kitten, lobster moth, yellow tail
birch	December moth, yellow tail, lackey, broad bordered yellow underwing
crab apple	eyed hawk, lappet, lobster moth, yellow tail
elm	comma butterfly, buff tip, gypsy moth, lackey, lime hawk
hawthorn	buff arches, vapourer, yellow tail, gypsy moth, lackey, pale oak eggar, December moth, oak eggar, lappet, lesser yellow underwing, broad bordered yellow underwing
hazel	lobster moth, buff tip, buff arches, lackey, vapourer, pale tussock
holly	holly blue butterfly
lime	buff tip, vapourer, lime hawk, December moth
oak	purple hairstreak butterfly, lobster moth, buff tip, pale tussock, yellow tail, gypsy moth, lackey, vapourer, December moth
poplar	poplar kitten, puss moth, white satin, poplar hawk, December moth, oak eggar
sallow	sallow kitten, puss moth, yellow tail, white satin, gypsy moth, eyed hawk, lappet, emperor, lesser yellow underwing, poplar hawk, lackey, broad bordered yellow underwing

willow	sallow kitten, puss moth, white satin, lackey, poplar hawk, lesser yellow underwing, broad bordered yellow underwing, lappet
blackthorn	vapourer, lackey, pale oak eggar, lappet, emperor, broad bordered yellow underwing
bramble	green hairstreak butterfly, buff arches, peach blossom, oak eggar, emperor, broad bordered yellow underwing
broom	silver studded blue, green hairstreak butterflies
buckthorn	brimstone butterfly, lappet
dog rose	yellow tail
dogwood	holly blue, green hairstreak butterflies, oak eggar
gorse	silver studded blue, green hairstreak butterflies
heather	silver studded blue butterfly, oak eggar, emperor
honeysuckle	broad bordered bee hawk
ivy	holly blue butterfly
privet	privet hawk
bedstraw	small elephant hawk, elephant hawk, humming bird hawk
bird's foot trefoil	common blue, dingy skipper butterflies
black medick	common blue butterfly
burdock	painted lady butterfly
charlock	green veined white, orange tip butterflies
chickweed	clouded buff, lesser yellow underwing, large yellow underwing
cuckoo flower (milkmaids)	green veined white, orange tip butterflies
dandelion	ruby tiger, clouded buff
deadnettles (purple and white)	garden tiger
dock	small copper butterfly, clouded buff, garden tiger
dog violet	small pearl bordered fritillary, pearl bordered fritillary, dark green fritillary, high brown fritillary butterflies
grasses	speckled wood, wall brown, marbled white, grayling, hedge brown, meadow brown, small heath, ringlet, chequered skipper, small skipper, large skipper butterflies, drinker
groundsel	wood tiger, cinnabar
hedge mustard	large white, small white butterflies
heartsease	pearl bordered fritillary butterfly, wood tiger

horse radish	large white, small white, green veined white butterflies
honesty	orange tip butterfly
jack-by-the-hedge	green veined white, orange tip butterflies
kidney vetch	small blue butterfly
plantain	wood tiger, clouded buff
ragwort	cinnabar
rest harrow	common blue butterfly
rock rose	brown argus, green hairstreak butterflies
storks bill	brown argus, green hairstreak butterflies
sorrel	small copper butterfly
spear thistle	painted lady butterfly
stinging nettle	red admiral, peacock, small tortoiseshell, comma butterflies
sweet violet	silver washed fritillary butterfly, wood tiger, broad bordered yellow underwing
scabious	narrow bordered bee hawk
willow herb	small elephant hawk, elephant hawk

Food of some exotic insects commonly kept in schools

common stick insect	privet
other available species of stick insect feed on	bramble
silkworms	lettuce, white mulberry
locust	grass

Giant Silkmoth larvae

giant emperor	plum, sloe, hawthorn
Tau emperor	oak, lime, beech
robin	willow, hawthorn, cherry
bull's eye	lime, cherry, willow
oak silkmoth	hawthorn, oak
American moon	walnut, birch
American ailanthus	privet, lilac, *Ailanthus*
European ailanthus	privet, lilac, *Ailanthus*
tree of heaven	privet, lilac, *Ailanthus*
Tussore silkmoth	oak
scarlet windowed	hawthorn, plum, sloe
southern Tussore	oak

golden emperor	vine, Virginia creeper
Indian moon	*Rhododendron,* hawthorn, plum
Edwards atlas	privet, willow, *Rhododendron*
giant atlas	privet, willow, *Rhododendron*
cherry	cherry, lilac, ash, birch

Flowers for butterflies

As well as providing food plants for larvae one needs to attract the adult insects. Flowers particularly attractive to butterflies include:

Buddleia	heliotrope
lilac	lavender
Aster (Michaelmas daisy)	honesty
Aubrietia	mignonette
Alyssum	*Petunia*
candytuft	primrose
catmint *(Nepeta)*	polyanthus
Centranthus	*Sedum spectabile*
cornflower	scabious
golden rod	sweet william
Hebe (Veronica)	*Verbena*

Insects living on common trees

The following list shows the number of insect species known to feed on various kinds of trees and so gives some idea of their potential for attracting insects:

oak	284	beech	64
willow	266	ash	41
birch	229	spruce	37
hawthorn	149	lime	31
poplar	97	hornbeam	28
crab apple	93	larch	17
Scots pine	91	fir	16
alder	90	holly	7
elm	82		
hazel	73		

Bees

Even where there is no intention of keeping bees, it might be wise to plant some plants known to attract bees to enable children to study the activities of these insects, for example:

The species of bees in school garden and proportions of each species.

The bees' relationship to flowers—what flowers do they work and how do they work them? Is there any obvious relationship between the colour and shape of flowers and the species of bees working them?

The habits of solitary bees; trap nesting them to study life cycle and parasites.

The habits of bumble bees, encouraging them to nest in nest boxes to study life cycles and population variations through year.

Weighing and measuring bees to show variations.

Study of pollen collecting apparatus of various species of bees.

The Bee Research Association gives extensive lists of trees and shrubs which encourage bees in a useful and inexpensive booklet, *Trees and Shrubs Valuable to Bees*, available from the Association at Hill House, Chalfont St Peter, Gerrard's Cross, Bucks.

The following list gives, in very abbreviated form, some of the information included in that publication. N indicates a source of nectar; P indicates a source of pollen.

Botanical name	Common name	Value to bees	
Shrubs			
Amelanchier	snowy mespilus		P
Berberis spp	barberry	N	P
Chaenomeles	Japanese quince	N	P
Cistus	rock roses	N	P
Colutea	bladder senna	N	P
Cornus alba	dogwood	N	P
Cotoneaster spp		N	P
Cytisus spp	brooms	N	P
Erica	heather	N	P
Escallonia		N	?
Fuchsia		N	P
Hypericum	St John's wort	?	P
Ilex	holly	N	P
Laurus	bay	N	?
Lavandula	lavender	N	P
Lonicera	winter-flowering honeysuckle	N	P
Mahonia		N	P
Mespilus	medlar	N	P
Olearia		N	P
Philadelphus	mock orange		

Potentilla fruticosa		N	P
Prunus laurocerasus	cherry laurel	N	P
Prunus lusitanica	Portugal laurel	N	P
Pyracantha	firethorn	N	P
Rhus typhina	stag's horn sumach	N	P
Ribes sanguineum	flowering currant	N	P
Rosa, single spp	roses (single)	?	P
Syringa	lilac	?	P
Tamarix	tamarisk	N	P
Ulex	gorse	N	P
Weigelia		N	?

Climbers

Parthenocissus	Virginia creeper, ampelopsis	N	P
Clematis montana		N	P
Hedera helix	ivy	N	P
Wistaria		N	P

Trees

Acer campestre	field maple	N	P
A. negundo	box elder	N	P
A. platanoides	Norway maple	N	P
A. pseudoplatanus	sycamore	N	P
Aesculus hippocastanum	horse chestnut	N	P
Ailanthus	tree of heaven	N	P
Alnus	alder	–	P
Betula	birches	–	P
Castanea	Spanish chestnut	N	P
Cercis	Judas tree	N	P
Crataegus	hawthorn	N	P
Fagus	beech	–	P
Fraxinus	ash	–	P
Liquidambar	sweet gum	N	?
Liriodendron	tulip tree	N	P
Malus	crab apples	N	P
Populus nigra	black poplar	–	P
Populus tremula	aspen	–	P
Prunus spp	almond	N	P
	wild cherry	N	P
	myrobalan plum	N	P
	bird cherry	N	P
	peach	N	P
	Japanese cherry	N	P
	blackthorn	N	P
Quercus	oaks	–	P
Robinia	false acacia	N	P
Salix	willow	N	P
Sorbus	whitebeam	N	P
	mountain ash	N	P
Tilia esp. *euchlora*	Crimea lime	N	P
Rosmarinus	rosemary	N	P
Senecio Greyi		?	P

Skimmia		N	P
Symphoricarpos	snowberry	N	P

Other flowers worth growing for bees include:
Hardy annuals

Alyssum	Californian poppy
Bartonia	*Godetia*
borage	*Lavatera*
candytuft	*Limnanthes*
Clarkia	mignonette
Coreopsis	nasturtium
cornflower	*Phacelia*
Cosmos (Cosmea)	scabious
Cynoglossum	shirley poppy
Echium plantagineum	sunflower

Half-hardy annuals

French marigold (single varieties for example,
Dainty Marietta, Naughty Marietta)
Mesembryanthemum

Hardy biennials

alkanet *(Anchusa officinalis)*
forget-me-not
wallflower

Herbaceous perennials

Achillea filipendula	*Helianthus*
Achusa italica	lemon balm *(Melissa officinalis)*
Aster (Michaelmas	
daisy)	bergamot *(Monarda)*
Bergenia cordifolia	catmint *(Nepeta mussinii)*
Campanula spp.	marjoram *(Origanum)*
Centaurea dealbata	*Pulmonaria*
Coreopsis	*Rudbeckia*
Doronicum	*Salvia superba*
globe thistle *(Echinops)*	*Scabious*
Erigeron	*Sedum spectabile*
Gaillardia	golden rod *(Solidago)*
Geranium	lamb's ears *(Stachys lanata)*
Geum	sea lavender *(Statice latifolia)*
Helenium	*Veronica spicata*

Rockery perennials

Arabis	rock rose *(Helianthemum)*
thrift *(Armeria maritima)*	perennial candytuft *(Iberis)*
Aubrietia	stonecrop *(Sedum acre)*
Campanula carpatica	thyme *(Thymus serpyllum)*

Homes for other small creatures

Old logs provide homes for many small creatures as well as fungi that live on the rotting wood.

The Devon Trust for Nature Conservation (2 Pennsylvania Road, Exeter EX4 6BQ) have produced a booklet, written by A. E. Stubbs and entitled *Wildlife Conservation and Dead Wood* (1972), which deals with the ecological value of dead wood. The following suggestions are adapted from that publication:

The following broad management ideals emerge for deciduous woodland:

1 A continuous supply of timber to be made available to maintain dead wood communities. In general there is no economic danger to a broadleaf forest in leaving dead wood of the same species; indeed it is an accepted silvicultural practice to leave unsaleable tops, branch-wood, etc., to rot.

2 Retention of unhealthy trees where there is no public hazard.

3 Diversity by maintaining a range of dead wood for each species of tree.

4 Diversity by including the four main types of dead wood listed by C. S. Elton in *The Pattern of Animal Communities* (Methuen, 1966), noting that a range in size is desirable.

Portions of all diameters of side limbs should be scattered around, in fact no part of the tree need be entirely removed, and an intact fallen tree is preferable to one fragmented. Piles of brushwood are regarded as good collecting grounds by coleopterists.

The fauna of even small pieces of dead wood can be large, a piece the size of a man's arm sometimes supporting fifty species, and in one survey a total of 231 species for logs 3 inches (7.5 cm) thick, lying on a woodland floor was found.

5 Trees should be allowed to reach the maximum size practical since a large body of dead wood can be expected to contain a greater diversity of niches and a more stable environment than a small log, and hence contain a richer fauna, including specialised species.

6   Natural shattered ends to logs and trunks, resulting from physical failure, are preferable to sawn surfaces.

7   Trunks should be cut so as to leave any existing holes low on the trunk which contain water.

8   Trees selected to be left as dead wood should be felled so as not to place them in situations of high exposure to sun or other climatic factors. It should be noted that fungal and animal populations of dead wood depend largely for their survival on a sheltered environment under woodland cover. Timber exposed to the sun suffers from heat sterilisation, and though some species are able to exploit such situations (for example certain solitary wasps), the normal sequence of decay is prevented and the large number of associated species are mostly absent.

9   Diversity by varying the environmental setting. This may include moderate exposure to sun under glade or edge conditions, but in such cases maintenance of an uncut field layer would help maintain humidity.

10   The need for flowers near to dead wood sites should be considered. Many beetles and diptera which breed in dead wood, are at least partially dependent on other habitats as adults. Flowers (herbs, shrubs and trees) provide an important food resource, especially hawthorn.

Sheets of corrugated iron, tiles, slates or asbestos sheets laid here and there will collect their complement of creatures. Most important, many creatures which normally live in the soil come to the surface in the darkness beneath the sheets and can thus be easily found and observed. Ants, for example, often build their nests in such situations. Piles of stones form nooks and crannies that may attract insects and spiders and perhaps small mammals. Plastic basins or dustbin lids or similar containers will form small pools, as mentioned in the section on ponds, which may be dispersed in different situations—sunlight and shade for example—and their complement of wild life compared. A manure or compost heap likewise will attract its own quota of plants and animals.

Economic pests

Not only are insects the largest group of animals, but they are of enormous economic importance, particularly those which are pests. So insect pests in the outdoor resource area are not just a nuisance but a useful teaching resource. The catalogue of common pests extends, of course, to other groups—slugs and snails, mites, millipedes, earthworms, eelworms and so on. With pests one can make observations of the growth and decline of populations during the year in quite a small area. Studies also might include examination of the effects of climatic factors, migration, colonisation, parasitism and hyperparasitism, predation, protective and warning coloration, life histories, overwintering methods, beneficial and harmful species, and chemical and other pest control methods. In particular, many pests offer opportunities for studying some of the interaction and interdependence found in ecosystems. For example:

Broad beans are almost certain to attract blackfly which in turn will probably be attacked by ladybird larvae and visited by ants. Brassica crops, especially Brussels sprouts, often harbour an interesting variety of insects; turnip flea beetles attack the seedlings; large white caterpillars on them are frequently heavily parasited by *Apanteles* which may be hosts for hyperparasites. These caterpillars have warning coloration whereas those of the small white butterfly which may appear on the same plant have protective coloration. These plants also may have cabbage aphis on them with their predators such as ladybirds and their larvae and hoverfly and horsefly larvae. They are frequently parasitised by *Aphidius*. The roots often harbour the cabbage root fly.

Slugs attack a very wide range of plants. Lettuce and French beans are favourites.

N. W. Runham and P. J. Hunter in *Terrestrial Slugs* (Hutchinson University Library, 1970) list the susceptibility of potato varieties to slug attack as:

Very High	High	Medium	Low
Maris Piper	King Edward	Majestic	Pentland Falcon
Ulster Glade	Record	Pentland Dell	
	Pentland Crown		

It would be interesting to check this information and to compile data about pest resistance in other crop varieties. Apple trees are hosts to a wide variety of pests such as winter moths, codling moth, apple sawfly, apply blossom weevil and capsid bug and also harbour a variety of predators on pest species. They also often have the economically important red spider mite on them. Some of the pests mentioned are specific in that they attack only one species. Others, like the slugs, feed on a wide range of crops.

Other common pests worth studying in the school grounds where the necessary host plants are grown include:

Specific feeders
Onion fly and carrot fly (both offer opportunities to study the ways in which the pests find their hosts and the ways of camouflaging the smell of the crops to 'mislead' the insects).
Bulb fly of wheat.
Leaf curling aphis on plums.
Raspberry beetle (the larvae of which are the white grubs found in the fruit, while the adults are readily found in the flowers as small brown beetles).

Pests of timber
Elm bark beetle, the vector for Dutch elm disease.
Pine weevil in conifers.
Giant wood wasps which tunnel into the heartwood of conifers and are parasitised by the ichneumon wasp *Rhyssa*.

Root feeders
Cranefly, or daddy longlegs, the larvae of which are the leatherjackets found in turf. In autumn the adults are often seen emerging from their pupae and flying up from lawns.
Cockchafer beetle or May bug, a large brown beetle with lighter coloured stripes which is found flying during May, usually in the evening and beneath trees. Their larvae are the thick, white curled grubs found in the soil which feed on plant roots. They are particularly fond of lettuce roots, eating them off and causing the lettuce to wilt.

Although we are concerned with insects and similar small animal life here, it should be noted that the study of plant disease offers no less opportunity for ecological study.

Some other features

Changes area

Most of this paper about the school estate emphasises building-up, developing and maturing, but equally essential are the processes of natural destruction which break down organic materials when they reach the end of their usefulness. Thus the changes of developing organisms, for example the seed becoming a seedling and the seedling changing into a mature plant, are clearly seen while destructive changes which reduce plant and animal tissue to the elemental material from which they come are less obvious.

While destructive changes can be discovered all over the estate, they are such an important part of the whole natural cycle that they deserve a special feature where pupils can study them in some detail. This is likely to be aesthetically unattractive and so it should be situated where the process is not obvious and where any smells of decay will not be offensive, as far as possible from neighbouring houses and the school buildings. It could be hidden within a wild area or screened by a hedge.

Just as plant and animal studies involve examining the stages of development of the organisms, so the studies in the changes area will involve observing stages of decay. It is possible for students to record changes and compare past records with the present situation but it is probably better to have several of the same features at these different stages. Thus several logs of similar timber, in varying states of decay will enable pupils to see the colonisation and succession of the timber by organisms of decay, in particular the fungi. It should not be difficult to achieve this stage if pieces of timber are deposited at intervals. See 'Homes for other small creatures', page 90.

Several compost heaps or bins will provide opportunities to investigate and compare the conditions required for fungal and bacterial decay and for measuring rates of change. The effects of adding soil, lime and a nitrogen source could be compared. The contents of the heaps or bins eventually will be useful on the cultivated areas.

Composting by accepted methods will demonstrate the way in which the natural process of decay is managed to produce a useful product for the garden or farm.

Other features for the changes area are:

Some piles of typical consumer litter, for example paper, clothing, plastics, various pieces of metal (for rusting and other forms of oxidation) and possibly an old mattress. If several piles of different ages could be arranged the degree of the degradibility of various forms of litter would be obvious.

Horse and sheep droppings and cowpats for examining the ecological succession in the decay of animal faeces.

A piece of dog meat to observe the chain of large organisms from blow flies to carrion and sexton beetles which depend upon the carcases of animals for their life cycle.

Piles of brushwood, litter from the floor of a wood, old turves and a straw bale left to develop fungi.

The decay of different kinds of material under observation might be compared in a variety of situations, for example upon or in the soil, isolated from the soil on a sheet of metal or asbestos, or kept dry under some sort of shelter.

Animal tracks

A richly planted school estate after snowfall will show a surprising number of bird and animal tracks. Such tracks are intensely interesting clues to the behaviour of animals as well as telling us a great deal about animal movement. Some very good books, such as F. J. Speakman's *Tracks, Trails and Signs* (Bell), help us to an understanding of the behaviour which has produced the tracks. Unfortunately, tracks in snow are usually fleeting and weather conditions are not conducive to spending much time studying them in detail.

The use of sand trays and mud spreads enables tracks to be recorded at almost any time of the year. Placed near bird feeding points, baited to attract small mammals or set at junctions or on paths which animals are suspected to travel, they could provide the basis for much interesting study.

The sand tray is simply a shallow tray of a convenient size, say 60 cm × 45 cm, which is filled with fine, soft, slightly-moist sand or sieved soil. It may be set into the ground, flush with the surface, as a semi-permanent feature so that shy animals become accustomed to it and do not avoid it. When it is to be used, it is a simple matter to smooth the surface with a ruler and look for results the next morning. Tracks in sand or soil are easy to cast in plaster, if this is desired. The trays can be lifted and carried inside for studying if this seems expedient.

A bird feeding table set within a broad tray of smooth sand is a simple way of making bird tracks available.

The mud spread is simply a fairly liquid mud mixed in a bucket and poured on the ground. If it does not spread easily it can be trowelled as one would spread cement. Within a short while, some of the water will have drained and evaporated out of the mud to give a consistency which will retain tracks made in it. Depending on the weather, the consistency will remain satisfactory for some hours, say overnight, before the mud hardens too much to take tracks.

Vivaria

Varied planting on school estates will attract a fairly rich insect and bird life and a pond and marsh garden will provide for fish, water insects and some amphibians. A few small mammals may appear in the grounds but for detailed mammal studies some form of small livestock housing will be required. Reptiles may be housed in a similar way but a more natural method of keeping both native and introduced reptiles, and some other animals, is to build an outdoor vivarium. This consists essentially of a wall surrounding an area, possibly with a moat about 45 cm wide just within the wall. A wall 1 metre high is adequate but it requires a capping which overlaps the inside by several inches to make escape difficult for any animal which may get across the moat and scale the wall. A minimum size of 3 m × 2 m is suitable, but the larger the space within the wall and moat, the more balanced and natural the reptile habitat may become. The space can be landscaped with caves and other secluded areas for the animals and with grass, plants and small shrubs.

Obviously, harmful animals such as venomous snakes or aggressive species, which may persistently attack others in such a confined space, will be avoided, but native slow-worms, lizards and toads (it is doubtful whether the space is large enough for fully-grown grass snakes except on a temporary basis) will provide material for handling and close study as well as for behavioural observation while in the 'natural' habitat. Some native reptiles are on the danger list for extinction, particularly the sand lizard and the natterjack toad, and care should be taken *not* to collect these unless the vivarium is suitable for breeding.

Trapping animals

Earlier reference was made to light-trapping insects and the dangers to rare or local species. Similar considerations apply to trapping all animals if we are to respect living organisms and demonstrate such respect and care for conservation to pupils. The main principles should be to trap only when there is clear need for it and to trap in such a way that the animals can be released after study. The two main reasons for trapping are to confirm the presence of species and to make population counts. In each case, if the animals are trapped by means which do not damage them, they can be released again shortly after capture.

   The outdoor resource area could be developed to provide opportunities for:

Netting using kite nets or sweep nets for collecting insects and similar creatures. The kite net is used for catching insects on the wing while the sweep net is passed over plants to gather any insects in its path.

Netting to collect organisms of ponds and streams. The dredge net is used as a sweep net in water, the trawl net is dragged by ropes across a pond or stream or behind a boat on rivers while the plankton net has a mesh bag with a glass tube at the end for collecting small organisms and gathering them into the tube.

Beating using a large beating tray of dark-coloured cloth stretched over a frame, or by laying a sheet of similar cloth on the ground, beneath a bush or tree which is beaten or shaken to dislodge insects, spiders and other animals.

Extracting from soil or litter by heating the material, usually by suspending it over a funnel and heating from above so that the organisms crawl away from the heat and fall into a container beneath, or floating animals from soil by immersing it in water in a shallow dish.

Pootering using a pooter to suck up individual insects and similar small animals. The pooter consists of a short length of wide (2 cm or so) glass tube fitted at each end with a cork and short lengths of narrower tube, to one of which is attached a piece of rubber tube. It is used by putting one end over an animal and sucking at the rubber tube to draw it into the trap. A piece of gauze over the inner end of the sucking tube avoids the risk of drawing animals from the trap into the mouth.

Pitfalling using a jam jar sunk to its rim in the soil to trap running insects. Cover the jar with a flat stone or a piece of wood to keep out rain and larger animals which might eat the insects, raising the top enough to allow the insects to pass under. Bait, such as meat, in the jar will attract scavenging insects.

Baiting using pieces of carrot, potato or turnip buried in the soil to attract millipedes, wireworms, woodlice, etc. Skewer the bait with a stick which protrudes above the ground to mark its position.

Catching small mammals using Longworth traps. These are baited with some suitable food such as bread or biscuit. It is a good idea to bait the trap for several days with the entrance locked open so that the animals become used to it before setting the trap to make a catch. Being metal, the traps are cold and small creatures may suffer from exposure. This can be avoided by putting some bedding such as hay in the trap and by examining the trap first thing each morning.

Livestock keeping

If livestock are to be kept they need to be adequately housed and accommodation ranging from an animal room for small creatures to specialised housing such as deep litter poultry houses, pigstyes and even loose boxes is provided in some schools. The subject is beyond the scope of this book, but since the outdoor resource area may be used for grazing some of this stock, and since some animals can be kept without permanent buildings, they are briefly mentioned here.

Some animals may be penned in mobile housing which is moved over grass for the animals to graze. Rabbits and guinea pigs may spend many months of the year in Morant hutches, being moved daily to fresh grass. Bantams and larger breeds of poultry thrive in fold units which are similarly rotated over grass. Goats and geese require night shelter and protection from bad weather and this can be given by housing on wheels which can be moved about the site as required. The goats may be tethered so that they have some freedom to browse and to reach their shelter but are restrained from wandering into areas where they may do damage. Geese generally require some wire fencing to keep them within bounds, although in one school they have the freedom of most of the school grounds, the school garden being fenced off to keep them out. In this circumstance, they present something of a problem due to their droppings which are left on paths and on playing space. Geese and other poultry may become the prey of foxes and dogs so it is important that night shelters and fold units should be predator-proof and that the birds should be locked in each night. A few schools keep sheep on the site and it is important to have adequate grassland for these and to pen them with a secure sheep wire and post boundary.

Apart from direct animal studies, livestock kept in this sort of accommodation can contribute to broader ecological studies of managed production systems. Thus rabbits, geese and sheep may be used for grazing studies. Geese have a further useful purpose as watch dogs where vandals are a problem.

The pond

Children are attracted by water and few features of the school estate create as much interest as a pond. It can be a thing of beauty

in itself, can be a compact and independent balanced ecosystem, can hold a tremendous variety of living things and can also be a valuable resource for the study of water itself. Yet experience shows that of all the features in the school estate the pond is often the most talked about and least used. The traditional and most permanent way of making a pond is to use concrete. In some school circumstances where a hard, impenetrable lining is essential, concrete may be the best material. However, this is a costly and time-consuming construction and permanence is not necessarily the most desirable quality.

The requirements for a pond as a study resource are the encouraging of as wide a range of plants and animals as possible (some will appear but the introduction of some ornamental pool plants as well as wild plants and water organisms is often desirable) and as little disturbance from cleaning as possible so that the plants and animals can achieve a natural balance. Scores of schools which have been provided by their architects with a biology pool in the wrong place, or of an unsuitable goldfish-pool design, have discovered to their cost the limitations of a too permanent or too formal and sterile design. It may be better to be in a position to change one's mind, to make mistakes and put them right again, than to have inflexibility.

Nowadays with the easy availability of wide polythene and PVC sheets and specially designed butyl rubber sheet liners, a pond can be made easily and quickly, with little more effort than that required to excavate the hole. Lining material may be obtained from a local garden shop, a specialist water gardening firm or one of the plastics suppliers advertising in the gardening press. It is worth a little initial care with levelling a site to avoid ending with a pond which appears to have water lower on one side than the other due

plan for a pond

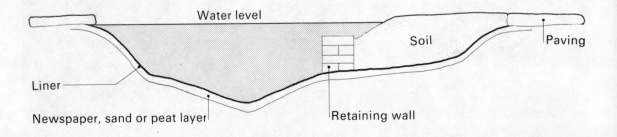

Water level

Soil

Paving

Liner

Newspaper, sand or peat layer

Retaining wall

to a slight slope of the ground in which it is set. The easiest way is to level (with pegs, a board and a spirit level) an area of ground a little larger than the space to be occupied by the pond, before beginning to excavate. If this level is prepared 5 cm lower than the final intended level of the surround, the polythene edges will be in the right place for covering by a 5 cm thick paving slab surround to the pond. Such initial preparation will make it easier to secure the paving slabs so that they are firm and do not rock when children stand on them.

The pond need not be deep. A deepest point of 50 cm will provide sufficient depth for the larger water plants and for enough unfrozen water for fish to survive severe cold spells. A range of depths as shown in the diagram will provide for a greater variety of plants and animals needing different depths. Slope the sides of the excavation fairly shallowly for this makes lining simpler and the edging of paving slabs more secure.

Since with plastic the effort and expense is so much less than that required with concrete it is much easier to make a reasonably sized pond, say of the order of 2 m × 2 m. Where space allows, 2 m × 2.5 m or 3 m has advantages.

When the excavation is complete, remove any sharp stones, roots, etc., which might puncture the plastic and line it with a good thickness of peat or soft sand. Alternatively, success has been achieved in ponds now several years old using up to 2.5 cm of wet newspaper. One of the best ways to do this is to wear Wellington boots, have a gently running sprinkler on a hose and put down layers of newspapers, wetting and treading them as you go. Put down as much paper as you can. The paper will form a soft base for the plastic and will absorb any stones which subsequently may work up through the soil.

This feature will be made more interesting and useful by coupling with it a marsh area so that pond and marsh blend together into a water garden. To do this it is necessary to extend the pond excavation to include the marsh area and to line the whole with newspaper and plastic liner, building a dry retaining wall at a convenient point. The marsh area is then back-filled with soil behind the retaining wall, as the diagram shows, before filling the pond.

Use heavy gauge 500 or 1 000 grade polythene sheet, which is available in widths up to 7 m, 0.014 grade PVC sheeting or a butyl pool liner. It is sometimes recommended that a double layer of polythene should be used as an additional safeguard against leaking. In fact the two thicknesses bond together tightly under the pressure of water to form an almost welded layer so that if a stick or a stone punctures the top layer it will almost certainly puncture the second layer. If you wish to use two layers, put down the first, add another 1 to 2 cm layer of wet newspaper, soft sand or peat and then put down the second polythene layer. Either black, blue or clear polythene may be used, but black is perhaps the least obtrusive in appearance. When ordering polythene, state that it is for a pond and be very careful about folding and handling; the smallest pinprick will lead to a leaking pond and these tiny holes are difficult to find. So fill the pond and check for leaks before putting the edging slabs down.

When measuring the excavation for the size of liner to order, lay a string across the largest dimension of the hole, lowering it so that it touches the sides and bottom all the way across. Cut the string at the edges of the pond, remove it, measure its length and add 60 cm. This will give you the length of the sheet required. Repeat the measurement at right angles to the first measurement; do not forget to add 60 cm. This measurement is the width of sheet required.

When laying the liner do not be too concerned about a smooth finish. Run the hose into the pond and the weight of water will push the plastic to the contours of the hole and any folds will, in time, become flattened so that they are almost invisible to even close inspection. It is better to let the plastic fold naturally under the weight of water than to try to make the folds yourself and risk damaging it, although where large folds occur there is no harm in helping the water to push them into their natural position.

When the pond is completely filled with water, trim surplus plastic away with scissors or a sharp knife but leave an overlap over the surface of the ground of 15 to 20 cm which will be held in place and covered by the paving-slab edging. The slabs should be large so that they overlap the water by about 4 cm, but do not tilt when children stand on the edge to work. Rectangular slabs are most generally useful but large, irregular pieces of broken slab, while more difficult to arrange, give a more informal effect which may be preferable in some circumstances. An even more natural finish may be achieved, if the site is in the natural area, by turfing up to the edge of the pond and over the plastic overlap.

Prefabricated glass fibre ponds are another possibility. They can be established very quickly. They are available in a variety of shapes and sizes but are usually small and relatively expensive.

The pond is not intended as a formal goldfish pool but is required to become as natural-looking and as varied in the life it contains as possible. It should be encouraged to become overgrown around the edges (keeping a clear space so that the children can get to it) so that it soon begins to look like a natural pond instead of something constructed from plastic. An initial stocking with some bottom rooting, floating and marginal plants with some waterside plants in the marsh and fish such as carp, rudd, tench and golden orfe will start off the colonisation of the water garden. Apart from these, the more organisms collected from natural ponds and introduced the better. This is not a purist aquarist's pool and while some of the introduced organisms may not settle down and survive, many will and will soon achieve a natural balance of plant and very varied

using a glass-bottomed bucket to observe life in a polythene-lined pond

animal life. There will be periods of cloudiness of the water but it is essential that these be left to disperse naturally and that attempts to drain the pool and start again are not made.

Water plants vary in their habits from those which root in the bottom and have aerial leaves which float or are held above water, to those bottom-rooters which have submerged leaves, to those which float freely with roots trailing in the water. A selection including each type is desirable and suitable species are listed in most catalogues from nurserymen specialising in water garden plants.

In addition to a pond/marsh watergarden, the school estate will be enriched by including small puddles or pools in various parts of the natural areas which will provide habitats for other organisms that spend all or part of their lives in water and which would not necessarily thrive in the pond. Such puddles and pools can be constructed from small pieces of polythene on the lines suggested for the pond or from old sinks or washbasins. Established in a variety of situations they will allow comparison of the living things which use water under different conditions, for example, light and shade.

While one prefers to leave a pond open, there are some situations where aesthetic considerations must be sacrificed for safety reasons or to maintain the pond in an educationally-useful state against interference. Thus where the pond is in a very vulnerable position there may be a risk in some situations of unauthorised entry to school grounds and the danger of small children falling in or of rubbish and stones being thrown in. A strong wooden framework covered with chainlink mesh which can be set over the pond when school is not in session will offer some protection. It requires locking with padlocks to at least two pieces of heavy gauge angle iron driven at least 60 cm into the ground with a few centimetres protruding to take the lock through a drilled hole. Such a grid cannot be used where tall water plants are growing.

For younger children especially the availability of a pond might lead to a much more adventurous approach to the study of water than is usually possible. A pond might become a port with ships and floating docks and all sorts of experiments with floating and sinking, wave patterns, stability, streamlining and many other topics being investigated in an exciting, practical way. Perhaps the pond could lead to a miniature river with rapids and waterfalls and banks being eroded, locks would have to be built to enable ships to negotiate these obstacles; a dam might seem necessary with a water wheel both to show how water power was first used and to lead on to consideration of the modern turbine. If the dam were in a suitable place it might be possible to use the water to set out a miniature irrigation scheme—why not on part of the vegetable garden, so that the effects of irrigation could be seen and crops on irrigated and non-irrigated land compared on a tiny scale involving 1.5 to 2.5 square metres.

All this may sound ambitious but it can be done and indeed generations of country children have dammed streams, built bridges, carried water along artificial canals and so on without anyone having to tell them what to do.

The cultivated area

The use of this area

The resource area will need to contain some limited space in which children can experiment with soils, growing plants, studying plant pests and diseases and weeds, and so on. The area will be an outdoor laboratory but, at the same time, it ought to give opportunities for the sheer joy of growing things.

The school garden in the past frequently did not often give much joy; too often children had to work hard to grow crops they were not very interested in and which were eventually sold to somebody else. We certainly do not want to go back to that situation. Nevertheless, many children do enjoy cultivating plants when they have a say in what is grown and some chance to enjoy, literally, the fruits of their labours. Thus, the cultivated area should be a purposeful resource in the pupils' eyes, where they can carry out experiments which their studies suggest and where they can try their hand at growing the plants which they become interested in during the course of their work.

At all costs schools must avoid using cultivated areas as school fund-raising resources, where crops are grown for sale. Equally, the desire to present neat rows of well-grown vegetables or formal park-type flower bedding schemes as show pieces for the school must be resisted. Fund-raising or show objectives usually lead to using the pupils as labourers and, while this suits a few, for most it is drudgery.

A major criticism of many school gardens in the past was that
they involved so much maintenance that the children spent most of
their time in dreary routine. They had little time for learning or
enjoyment. If this is to be avoided it is essential that the area be kept
down to the minimum that is necessary to do the job required. Plots
should be as small as is consistent with the objectives in view,
narrow so that much if not all the plants can be reached from the
paths, and if possible edged so that they remain clearly defined with
a minimum upkeep. Concrete paving slabs are ideal for this edging.

Features in a cultivated area

In accordance with the policy of providing for the educational needs
of pupils, and incidentally reducing maintenance problems, the
cultivated area should consist chiefly of small plots for experimental
work and just growing things. While we suggest that the variety of
life and of ecological situations which flower borders and garden
shrub grouping provide can be found in the more natural areas (there
is no reason why garden flowers and shrubs should not occur in the
natural areas), it may be desirable in some school grounds to create
borders and groupings as decorative features. These will have to be
arranged according to the site and situation but there is a plethora of
books to help here.

The sort of facilities provided will be dictated by the educational
requirements of individual schools and since our purpose here is
merely to deal with the provision of features, space does not allow
description of the educational uses of the area. Some of the possibilities are described in the books listed on p. 151. The books published
for the Nuffield Secondary Science, Nuffield Combined Science,
Nuffield O-level Biology and Science 5/13 Projects refer to numerous
experiments to be carried out in a cultivated area. Obviously cultivated areas should be on the best soil available and drudgery should
be taken out of their preparation and maintenance by using mechanical cultivators.

Chequerboard gardens

One response to the problem of maintenance has been the development of paved gardens, now usually called chequerboard gardens.
Although these have been in use in some schools for many years,

they have only recently been adopted widely. The idea is simply that, particularly with the younger children, what is wanted is a lot of very small plots instead of a few large ones. Since the area of a 60 cm × 60 cm paving slab makes a perfectly adequate tiny plot, a complex of plots and paths can be provided very simply by paving an area with slabs of this size, missing out every other slab in chessboard style. This gives an area in which:

Access is easy.
Every bit of cultivated ground can be reached by children from a hard path.
Maintenance is easy. Paths and edges are maintenance free; cultivated areas are kept to a minimum.
The number of little plots helps to organise a variety of work.
The layout can be changed easily according to the needs of the moment.
Any available size of slabs can be used but 60 cm × 60 cm × 5 cm slabs have a number of advantages. They are reasonably light and easy to handle; they are cheaper per unit area than the thicker 60 cm × 90 cm slabs; and their size is convenient for both plots and 'paths'.

The area available for growing plants may seem trivial. However, each small plot is the equivalent of greenhouse bench space which would hold sixteen 15 cm pots or sixty-four 7.5 cm pots, so it is not to be despised. Each of these little plots could hold a group of flowers, or several small groups. It could hold enough vegetables for most class purposes—perhaps only one potato or Brussels sprout, but six or eight onion plants, a dozen carrots, five or six lettuces and so on. They would be adequate for many of the experiments carried out by older children, for example, randomised plot trials, the raising of material for more specialist study by fifth- and sixth-formers. Of course there is an infinite variety of designs possible, using just this one basic unit. Plots do not have to be 60 cm × 60 cm. They can be 60 cm × 120 cm, 120 cm × 120 cm and a variety of more or less complicated shapes and sizes.

It is well worth while going to some trouble to get the area for the chequerboard garden prepared to begin with. The space to be used should be thoroughly cleaned of weeds, by fallowing if necessary, and should be dug and then raked down to give a perfectly flat, firm surface. If the soil is not very fine, a centimetre or two of sand or ashes spread over the surface will help to provide a level base for the slabs. It will also deter slugs which may collect under the slabs. It is probably wisest to lay sand over the whole area to get a large level surface, lay the slabs and then scoop most of the sand out of the plots, forking in any which remains.

If the chequerboard is to be set in mown grass it should be arranged to give a finished paved surface flush with the grass area to ease mowing. If the result is to be an attractive and workmanlike job, it is essential to get an accurate layout, starting with a good straight edge and an exact right angle in the corner.

The use of pesticides

Where pesticides are used, they must be used with care and be seen to be used carefully, so that the pupils are given an example of responsible use of these chemicals. This applies to the selection and use of chemicals by ground maintenance staff as well as in the cultivated area. A code has been prepared by a joint committee of the British Agrochemicals Association/Wild Life Education and Communications Committee, with representatives of the Ministry of Agriculture, and published as *Pesticides: A Code of Conduct* (available from B.A.A., Alembic House, 93 Albert Embankment, London, S.E.1 7TU). Under the heading 'Role of gardeners' the following responsibilities are listed:

1   to select the correct pesticide for the job,
2   to read the instructions carefully and follow them rigorously,
3   to check quantities and not add 'one for luck',
4   to handle all pesticides with care and store both full and partly used containers out of the reach of children; to keep pesticides away from pets, including fish,
5   to avoid spraying plants in open blossom (otherwise bees, for example, may be killed),
6   to avoid spraying in windy weather to prevent injuring or contaminating other plants or drifting into neighbouring gardens,
7   to wash out watering cans and sprayers thoroughly after the use of pesticides and avoid washings draining into water courses and ponds,
8   to dispose of used containers safely by thoroughly washing out whenever possible and placing them in a dustbin,
9   to wash immediately after using pesticides.

The same care needs to be exercised in the use of fungicides and herbicides.

Soil studies

A resource area that had cultivated plots, mown grass, rough grass, conifers and deciduous trees would provide plenty of opportunity to study the soil under various kinds of vegetation, arable and grassland conditions with various fertiliser and liming regimes. Other aids to soil study might be:
Soil profile trench A trench 60 to 90 cm deep would allow examination of the top soil and subsoil. It would need to be quite large (at least 75 cm wide) if more than a cursory examination is to be made. In some soils, space for frequent refacing of the profile would be necessary and slabs or boards would need to be used round the edge to prevent crumbling. Where there is a high water table there would be a danger of flooding, but studies in variation of water table might possibly be something of a compensation for this.

Some schools have a series of 'watertable holes' around the site, in which the depth of water may be measured by a stick. For the sake of safety the excavation should be surrounded by a fence of some sort.

Root study trench This would probably be incorporated in the soil profile trench. The idea is to make it possible to observe the growth of roots and activities of worms and other soil creatures. An open, exposed surface will not allow this because of drastic alterations to light and moisture conditions. So what is needed is a vertical soil surface covered by a sheet of strong glass which in turn can be covered by a sheet of marine plywood or some other rotproof material to exclude light. Car window glass from a car breaker's yard is cheap and very suitable. The plywood cover can be removed when observations are to be carried out.

Soil aspect bank An earth bank with sloping sides facing north and south would enable studies to be made of the effects of soil temperature and other microclimatic factors of slope and aspect. Such a bank of 2 to 2.5 m length can be built by erecting walls of brick or stone to support the end of a slope. Lay a course of bricks or stones about 2 m long running north and south. Lay a similar one, parallel and 2 to 2.5 m away. Add further courses to each wall, reducing the length of each course to achieve triangular shaped walls rising about 60 cm from ground level to apex. Fill the space between the walls with soil to provide a bank with north and south facing slopes. Alternatively a pyramid of soil, say 2 m square and 1 m high in the middle could be used. Whatever the type chosen, it must be situated so that it is free from shading.

Erosion table This is usually part of a specialist geography room, but outside it is possible to construct one on a larger scale, which would be much more exciting and effective in use and would also save valuable classroom space. Water would have to be available but a length of hose would supply this.

Weather studies

If it is simply a statistic-gathering exercise weather recording is sterile and meaningless to all but the statistically-minded. However, if records are kept to be used to help explain various aspects of plant and animal behaviour, or to see the effects on everyday life, or even to forecast trends or imminent weather conditions then they can be meaningful and intensely interesting.

The extent of variation of weather conditions determines the behaviour of many plants and animals. Thus heavy rainfall in June (unusual in most years) when day length and sunlight intensity are at their highest produces particularly vigorous plant growth even among slow-growing hardwood trees; low temperatures in May prevent insects flying and thus reduce the pollination and setting of fruit blossom; several weeks of drought in August cause grass leaf growth to almost cease while a wet August means a need for very frequent lawn mowing; mild winters mean the survival of a large over-wintering insect population and aphids, wasps and other insects are particularly numerous in the following summer.

To a more limited extent there is value in observing weather developments, for example changes in pressure, relative humidity and wind direction as a means of forecasting changes in the weather. Local observations, coupled with the information about wider weather readings and weather phenomena, such as Atlantic cyclones and anticyclones as put out by the Meteorological Office through television, radio and the newspapers lead to understanding the cause of weather conditions, forecasting techniques and the factors which determine the climate we have.

For recording of general weather conditions over the locality a small weather station set in a fairly open position is needed. A rain gauge, a wet and dry thermometer and a maximum and minimum thermometer are the main requirements. The thermometers should be protected from direct sunlight but must have a free flow of air around them. A Stevenson screen or some modified louvred box is the best way to provide protection and free air-flow. A barometer in the school will give pressure readings and the only other device needed is something for recording wind direction from time to time; a simple wooden or tinplate wind vane will suffice. If wind speeds are required, the Beaufort landsman's scale will give reasonable indications. Alternatively, a hand held anemometer made from four halves of table tennis balls or a large one made from four halves of ballcock floats or the cones from the top of plastic squeezy bottles will do. Paint one of the cups a bright colour so that the revolutions can be counted easily and calibrate the revolutions per minute against the Beaufort scale or against a borrowed hand anemometer such as Air Force stations, some colleges and, indeed, some schools have and which you may be able to borrow.

Many more interesting weather studies can arise from investigating and comparing microclimates on the school grounds; that is looking at variations between, say the north and the south side of a bank, under trees and in the open, or over grass and bare soil and relating the observations to the growth and behaviour of living things. Much of this can be done by direct observation, i.e. looking to see where the frost lies thickest, where it thaws most rapidly, where no frost appears on a frosty morning and by following this up by looking at the effect upon plants and animals: for example which plants are killed by frost and which are not obviously frost-damaged? Much of this work requires no more apparatus than the human eye, but for recording when pupils cannot be present, or to get more accurate measurements of conditions, some simple apparatus is required.

So the school estate provides useful opportunities for weather study, but effort spent on considering weather in general is less meaningful and useful than that spent on finding out about what weather variations mean to us and to the plants and animals around us. Thus it is all the influences of weather, profound and trivial, that make the study of weather by pupils important in school and these studies are an essential part of all children's environmental education. Weather studies based on impacts such as the following may be explored and developed more thoroughly through access to resources in the school grounds:

the influence of weather on sporting and game activities,
the creation of artificial climates, both in glasshouses and out-of-doors by artificially influencing temperature, light and water supply,
weather and visibility,
weather and drying,
keeping dry,
keeping warm and keeping cool,
sun movement,
weather and food.

Our painters and writers have a lot to teach us here—'Season of mists and mellow fruitfulness' is the familiar opening of Keats *Ode to Autumn.* Is autumn a misty season? How misty? How does visibility vary from day to day and season to season? What part of the day is misty? Is the mistiness natural or caused by smoke?

Another aspect worth studying in the school grounds is the use of climatic factors by man as a source of energy. All are familiar with the use of a 'burning glass' for condensing the sun's rays so that they burn paper. Beekeepers use the sun's rays to melt beeswax. Both these are examples of heat energy supply controlled by weather conditions.

A windmill is a simple machine providing a source of power depending upon weather conditions. It would not be difficult to set up on the school grounds. It could be based on a simple wind vane propeller with a driving belt to a cycle dynamo to generate electricity for lighting a bulb.

These two examples of weather as an influence upon man suggest the basis for many realistic studies in the physical sciences and the part of these principles in shaping our environment. The principles and applications range from the properties of air and its movement and pressure to the transmission of heat energy; from its effect upon materials to the influences of temperature and evaporation of moisture upon plant wilting. All these have direct and indirect effects on our lives.

An outdoor craft area

'As we watch any craftsman at work, whether it be the basket maker, the potter, or the blacksmith, we cannot fail to be struck, if we think about it, by the way the natural qualities of the raw materials —the springy willow rods, the moist, unformed clay and the tough, unshaped metal—have determined the nature and form of the articles we use in our everyday life.'

Schools and the Countryside (Department of Education and Science Education Pamphlet No. 35)

The usual school craft materials are standardised and choice is limited, while natural materials have infinite variety and so, in choosing them, children need to use and develop their powers of discrimination. The realisation that *that* piece of wood will best serve the purpose in mind demands some judgement where natural materials are concerned. On the other hand, the materials themselves sometimes suggest the use to which they might be put so that the realisation that *this* piece is just perfect for making a dog or a fish or whatever it may be brings into play an opportunism and imagination which ought to be worth cultivating.

Perhaps, too, in a culture that is so 'instant' and 'prepacked', we ought to let children see whenever possible our dependence on the earth for the materials we use. The point is that there is a justification for introducing traditional crafts into schools that lies in their real educational value and is not dependent on any sentimental desire to return to the past. Children get great pleasure from working with these materials. The besom, the rustic hanging basket, the sculpture from a piece of timber carved along its natural lines and smoothed and polished, the corn dolly, the dried material table decoration—all are far more satisfying to many children than a plastic model built from preformed pieces, a tube of glue and instructions thought up by someone else. It may be possible to set aside certain areas specially for producing craft material, for example some willow stools for basketry withies, borders for raising decorative material or plots for straw production, though where any quantity of material is needed it will have to be bought in.

Apart from providing examples of craft materials, the school estate could include a fenced off area where materials could be stored and where much of the work could be carried out. The fencing could be rustic or hurdles made as a craft activity and could enclose an open work space and a lean-to shelter (also built as a craft activity with, perhaps, a thatched roof) to protect the stored materials and the objects in the course of making. Apart from estate-produced material, the craft area could store bundles of rushes, logs for carving, materials for coppice crafts, clay for pottery and so on. Within the compound traditional craft tools could be erected, such as pole lathes, coppice craft vices and woven hurdle forms. The area could provide a centre for the school's craft work in raw materials, being a compact store and workshop and a centre of interest for both the more intellectual and the less able pupils.

3   Making use of limited space

The emphasis so far has been on school grounds which include open areas where free planting can take place. The grounds of many schools, in urban areas in particular, are severely restricted or non-existent. Nevertheless, ingenuity has created not only resources for teaching but a greatly improved school environment in some of these most unpromising situations. The best opportunity for development in most restricted sites lies in the courtyards and other spaces around the buildings.

Courtyards

Some newer schools have courtyards which form decorative areas enclosed totally or partially by the buildings. Sometimes they are extensive quadrangles where there are lawns with trees and shrubs or formal beds of flowers. Where space is more limited, the enclosure may be paved with slabs, cobbles or other decorative surfaces, with a few slabs or cobbles omitted here and there to give room for plants. Many of these courtyards and quadrangles are solely decorative, having been designed either as an integral part of the original conception of the whole school complex or as a means of dealing with odd areas which the addition of new buildings has left. Some teachers treat these spaces as outdoor extensions to the classroom where children can take chairs and books or other apparatus and carry out their activities in the open air in fine weather. Some go further and use the plants as material for study of various kinds from objects for drawing and painting, to sources for measuring activities or resources for nature study.

A number of schools have developed in these courtyards some of the features mentioned in the earlier sections, albeit on a smaller but more intensive scale. They have found it possible to introduce features with a great deal of educational potential even though large

making good use of the
courtyard—but don't leave
mowers with young
children!

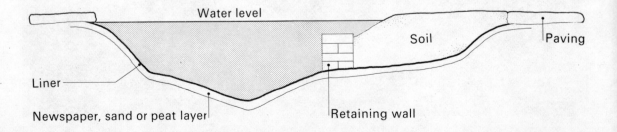

Soil

Liner

Animals maintained included:

rabbits (Netherlands dwarf, Polish, Dutch)
guinea pigs
ferret
border canaries and other small birds (all from
stocks bred in captivity)
Chinese painted quail
frogs; toads; newts—smooth, palmate and
crested
stickleback; ruffe, carp
slow-worms, grass snake, green lizards
Greek tortoise.

Many plants were grown, including:

tubs	*Lonicera, Clematis, Jasminum,* climbing roses
pond and marsh	many marginal plants and aquatics, including submerged and floating plants
terrarium	meadow turf—grazed regularly by guinea pigs
troughs	alpines—1 trough calcicole, 1 calcifuge, one scree
flower bed	assorted—including assorted cereal specimens, various experimental plots
greenhouse shelves	assorted cacti and succulents, including *Lithops* and other mimics, *Bryophyllum,* aloes, *Mammillaria, Cereus,* etc.
benches	assorted, including pelargoniums (many miniatures), *Poinsettia, Achimenes, Aralia, Beloperone, Campanula isophylla, Cissus, Coleus, Ficus, Grevillea, Hedera, Monstera* and many more
hanging pots	*Columnea, Platycerium,* Bromeliads
humid section	assorted Pteridophytes, Bryophytes, *Selaginella, Lycopodium,* epiphytic orchids and *Ficus pumila*
climbing (free below staging)	*Passiflora, Stephanotis*

Features for courtyards and roofs

Raised beds and borders

Sometimes it is possible to have asphalt or concrete surfaces and
their underlying base taken up and replaced by soil. However, this

is expensive and heavy work and may disturb drains and other services buried beneath them and create drainage problems, and is therefore a case for consultation with the architect's department. In some yards, if no danger to services exists, it may be desirable to plant trees as well as (or as an alternative to) providing beds and borders. Obviously the substrata below the hard surface must be suitable to support the growth of a tree. A superintendent of a city recreation department recommends that for tree planting a hole one metre square and one metre deep should be prepared with suitable soil in which to plant the tree and that, after planting, tree grates should be placed around the tree to prevent consolidation of the soil by children who will naturally gather around it.

Less drastically and more quickly, beds have been built direct on the hard surface by importing soil and containing it in low brick or concrete walls. Kerbstones are good for this and though they allow only a limited depth of soil, this will prove adequate for a reasonable variety of plants. Often the quantity of soil which can be obtained is only sufficient for shallow beds anyway.

Deeper beds can be built from bricks, preferably cemented together but leaving spaces between the bricks of the bottom course for drainage. This bottom course should be filled with rubble topped with a 50 to 75 mm layer of gravel or clinker before the soil is added to provide adequate drainage and to prevent the soil washing through the spaces in the bricks. As an added precaution against soil washing through, a layer of glass fibre roof-insulating material can be put on top of the gravel or clinker. Alternatively, use paving slabs set on edge and held in a rectangle by two heavy gauge wires which encircle them. The tension can be maintained with turnbuckle wire-strainers. Built up beds and borders can produce problems of watering and drainage. Adequate drainage material, as described above, will look after drainage difficulties but may speed the drying out of the bed in hot weather. Adequate organic matter (leaf mould, chopped turf or peat) in the soil will help to retain moisture but a supply of water nearby is essential in very dry weather.

Built up beds can affect the fabric of the buildings and it is important that, if sited against a wall, they do not rise above the damp-proof course unless a damp-proof shield is placed between them and the wall. Similarly, it is important that the beds should not cause drains to become silted up. Hence, it is wise to consult the people responsible for buildings maintenance before proceeding with such plans.

Some parks departments have constructed beds in school yards from old railway sleepers laid on their sides, one on top of the other, and held together with metal plates. They report that these have proved very satisfactory in tarmac yards.

Troughs, tubs and other containers

Where the permanence of beds and borders is not desirable or where the space available is inadequate, containers of various types have been used. These must be large and deep enough to contain sufficient soil to avoid the need for over-frequent watering. Experience shows that a minimum depth of 45 cm is desirable. Those containers which have shallow sloping sides are less satisfactory than vertical-sided ones for much of their surface has little depth of soil beneath it. Wooden tubs are increasingly difficult to obtain and concrete or glass fibre ones are more robust and require no maintenance. Cylindrical tubs are better than the tapered type because they hold a greater volume of soil and more depth overall. Old sinks are too shallow for most plants, but they make ideal miniature gardens for rockplants, seedling trees and other small subjects, provided they can be regularly and frequently tended.

Old chimney pots also make useful containers, particularly for plants which will trail over the side and hang down. The bottoms may be filled with several inches of rubble and, unless they are to be moved while filled, there is no reason to seal the bottom. Should a bottom be desired it can be made with cement, but push a few pieces of 25 mm dowel through to be withdrawn later to leave drainage holes. Hanging baskets have the advantage of not requiring ground space but they need a suitable and secure place for hanging. They are also very liable to be forgotten and to be left to dry out. Baskets should be as large as possible so that they hold a large volume of soil. Care must be taken if pupils have to stand on chairs or steps with cans of water to water them. If they are suspended on clothes line pulleys the pupils can raise and lower them to tend them more easily.

Traditional plant pots dry out rapidly in most yards and are best kept in a plunge bed. This consists of a frame of 225 mm boarding, set on the ground and filled with peat, sand or weathered ashes, in which the pots are buried up to their rims. By building up the walls of the frame so that the back is higher than the front, frame lights may be fitted to give protection during adverse weather for more tender subjects.

The watering of all containers is even more difficult than with raised beds and borders and arrangements for daily, and even twice daily, water are necessary in dry weather. Watering during school holidays, of both beds and containers is often a problem but unless arrangements can be made, the use of such facilities is severely limited.

Plants for beds, borders and containers

The plants grown will depend, as anywhere else, on what is required by way of teaching resources, bearing in mind that it is not merely the educational value of the plants themselves but also of the other organisms (insects and possibly birds) which they will attract. A second limiting factor is the exposure to draught and shading already mentioned and in non-smokeless zones, the degree of air pollution. As a starting point, observation of what thrives in neighbouring front gardens and window boxes may suggest suitable plants. The local parks superintendent may advise on suitable plants for the locality and may even prove to be a source of supply from his surplus material. By far the best way is to involve the pupils with trying to grow the plants which seem most likely to provide the resource they require and trying alternatives when failures occur, thus finding by trial and error what suits your purposes in your situation.

In terms of space, a 45 cm diameter tub will support a young tree for some years, for example an oak, a beech or a conifer. A similar container will hold a couple of cabbages, a potato, a sowing of wheat, a collection of climbers, for example one runner bean, one pea, one nasturtium, or the variety of bedding plants or bulbs one usually expects to find in such a container.

As the climbers mentioned above illustrate, these gardens do not depend solely on low growing plants. The variety may be extended by training plants upwards on trellises fixed to walls, stakes, brush-wood or trellis structures. Use of the vertical dimension is possible with the traditional strawberry barrel; a barrel of soil with holes cut in the side for planting. Many plants, apart from strawberries, can be grown in such a barrel. An adaptation of the barrel principle is a raised bed constructed in a pyramid pattern to give terraces of soil which permit more plant space than planting on a flat border.

Finally, wall tops, fitted with specially made wooden troughs, will grow plants which normally climb, for example nasturtiums and sweet peas, but which unsupported will trail down the wall although in all but windless sites the plants may suffer scouring on the wall surface and may be safer secured to trellis. Alternatively, a large wooden trough at the base of the wall will take climbing plants such as nasturtiums, sweet peas or even marrows or runner beans, if wires are fixed to the wall to support them. Even better than wires is a trellis of plastic-covered Weldmesh or heavy polythene mesh panels fastened to 50 mm×25 mm battens secured to the wall. With careful planning and choice of plants, an unattractive wall could become a place of colour and interest.

Ponds

A raised polythene, PVC, butyl rubber or even prefabricated glass fibre pond can be built within a brick or paving-slab raised bed. Another useful method is to use peat blocks to build a container, but, to avoid peat being distributed all over the yard, the whole pond area should be enclosed by 225 mm boards set on edge and screwed together to form a surround. One school built a pond by making a wooden framework the size and shape of the pool, its height, of course, corresponding with the required depth. Hardboard sheets were then nailed to this to support the plastic, which was then fitted inside and nailed to the top, after the pond had been filled with water (p. 130). It could be raised to table height. This is a particularly useful device for temporary use and has the advantage that they may be safer than lower ones in which small children can fall. The weight of water in a pond is considerable so it is not merely a matter of building the pond on a large table and so the supports beneath must be adequate.

Greenhouses

If a large enough space in a sunny position is available, a greenhouse will protect plants from wind currents between buildings, will allow a wide range of plants to be grown and will provide a place for raising pot plants for inside the school building and space where

such plants can revive after being subjected to classroom conditions. The benches on which the pots stand could be constructed on the capillary bench watering principle and would save a great deal of watering maintenance. A local parks officer would advise on the construction of such a bench but essentially it consists of a trough of sand which is constantly supplied with water by a ballcock or inverted poultry drinker system. The trough can be made from a batten frame fixed to the top of the bench and lined with sheet polythene. Builder's sand will be suitable for the bed. If pots and trays with large drainage holes are used with no broken crocks or other drainage materials in them and they are pressed firmly into the sand water will rise through the sand directly into the pot compost by capillarity. The only attention required is to fill the poultry drinkers as required or to ensure that the ballcock tank is constantly filled.

The school entrance hall

Some entrance halls are large enough to carry a jardinière of pot plants. Apart from displays of potted plants the trough may be used to create desert gardens with sand, rocks and potted cacti and succulents with their pots sunk and hidden in the sand. The trough lends itself to many other displays from harvest festival collections of fruit, autumn leaves, pots of cereals, geological specimens, zoo-logical material, indeed any display which has affinity with the living world and which benefits from the inclusion of living material.

A very large entrance hall can house a watergarden and a range of naturally arranged pot plants. Schools have achieved high standards of decoration and created pupil interest by using peat blocks and polythene to build ponds in which potted water plants have been sunk and fish introduced. Around this they have arranged loose, dry peat and rocks with potted plants, the pots being hidden in the peat. If you contemplate such a garden, put a layer of heavy gauge plastic on the floor first, and surround the whole garden with stones or some other border to prevent the peat being scattered by pupils looking at the feature.

It is important to site the hall garden in as draught-free a position as possible, and where it will receive the most light. In many newer schools this is easily achieved and only the dry, warm atmosphere from central heating may be a problem. This can be ameliorated to some extent by occasionally spraying over the plants with clear water. Older halls which are dark, draughty and dry may only sustain a limited range of plant species. Indeed, in most halls it is probably wise to look on gardens as temporary displays rather than as places where the plants can grow. This means that the garden needs the support of a greenhouse where plants can be put to recover. Indeed, plants which are sufficiently large to make a visual impact in entrance halls and foyers will probably have taken a long time to grow and will quickly deteriorate if they are not returned to good growing conditions after a spell on display in the hall. One further consideration when siting such gardens is to arrange them so that they do not impede the passage of pupils, particularly to fire exits.

Attracting animals to the courtyard

In a heavily built-up area one would not expect a large variety of insects and birds to be attracted to the plants introduced in beds and containers. Nevertheless, the plants will not remain pest-free and aphids and some butterfly and moth larvae may be expected. In addition, insects which prey on such plant pests, such as ladybirds and species of ichneumon, may appear. There is no reason why insect eggs and larvae should not be imported. Cinnabar larvae could be collected from ragwort and introduced to ragwort or groundsel growing in a trough. Eggs of red admiral or peacock butterflies can be bought from a supplier and can be hatched and the larvae transferred to a bed of nettles set up in a trough. One city school bought moon moth eggs and raised them to the adult stage in their greenhouse.

A variety of birds would not be expected in a densely urban school courtyard but a bird table set up in winter with a variety of food and a trough of water may attract some unlikely visitors. At least it will provide an opportunity for studying the feeding, drinking, bathing and social behaviour of house sparrows and starlings.

Captive small animals

Care must be taken about keeping animals in cages and hutches in draughty, sunless courtyards. A small wooden hut, sited in a position where some sun can reach the windows, would provide an animal house in which to keep such hutches and cages. Thus urban pupils would have the opportunity to learn about the needs and be- haviour of captive animals and their reliance on man. The animal house could house a variety of small mammals, reptiles and birds, or could be devoted to one group, for example guinea pigs.

Aviaries

Attractive cage birds are a delight to children and a number of schools have been able to make satisfactory aviaries in unpromising situations. One school did this with a tall, 2 m wide cupboard while another roofed over a courtyard between buildings with wire netting, as described earlier in the paragraphs on courtyards.

4   Administrative considerations

Programming design and development of outdoor resource areas

New schools

In designing a new school in which the entire site was a resource for education there is a need for some emphasis on certain considerations from the very beginning:

1 Planners need to consider the question of outdoor resource areas with all the other factors they now take into consideration when deciding where schools shall be sited. Thus, while rectangular flat surfaces are desirable for playing areas, they should also consider other possibilities. Such features as variety of slope, hedges and banks, ponds and streams, woodlands or mature trees, hedgerows, rough wasteland, quarries would all be worth incorporating.

2 When purchasing the site for a new school, land agents might examine their plans for the existence of odd parcels of land adjoining the proposed area. Often such parcels, because of their position, topographical nature or poor access, have little apparent value, but added to the proposed school grounds they may make an invaluable contribution to education. Some authorities already purchase such adjacent pieces of land for use as study areas or school nature reserves as part of a county conservation plan.

3 Where the education department prepares a general outline brief for the architects this should contain guidance about the broad requirements for the use of the site as an overall education resource.

4 Once the site is allocated, architects and landscape architects would need to develop their designs in the context of buildings set in a rich educational environment, rather than as a matter of buildings and playing fields with some landscaping for aesthetic purposes. Matters for particular consideration might include:

a Retaining existing features of educational value or of potential use such as hedges, open ditches and other watercourses, areas of copse, banks, undulating ground, etc.

b Planning outdoor features, grounds layout and planting for educational as well as amenity interest in the same way that the planning of school buildings is approached.

c Designing special buildings and facilities for environmental activities; obvious items are glasshouses and biology ponds.

d Accommodation for livestock and covered work spaces.

e Providing other special needs, for example open-air theatres and outdoor work space for artists, such as kiln sites.

f Supplying a variety of materials in and around the buildings, for example natural rocks such as slate, cobblestones, sandstones and man-made examples of rock texture.

g Paying particular attention to the siting of some special features such as cultivated areas which need to be reasonably close to buildings so as to be convenient for use and an obvious part of the educational facilities, secure from possible further extension of the buildings since many planted areas take a considerable time to mature their educational potential, sited where the soil is suitable, where the sun may reach and where, in exposed conditions, there is some protection.

h Looking beyond the present plan to likely sites for any extension building which may become necessary in the future. Such foresight would afford some security to outdoor features by enabling service lines to be sited to serve the future building. Extensions to buildings often obliterate outdoor features because their siting is determined by the position of service lines.

These conditions depend on the type of outdoor resources which teachers see as useful and how they wish to use them. In the first place, understanding of the full educational value of the outdoor resource area is developing and will grow rapidly as more teachers use the facility. At present there is little documentation of how the various school subjects can use the school grounds, except in the biological field. However, the extensive interest shown by schools, colleges of education and local education authorities indicates that this is a matter which will be resolved within a few years as ideas develop. Secondly, teachers who will use the facilities in any school being designed will not have been appointed by this early stage and will not be available for consultation. However, there are sources of professional expertise, in addition to that of local authority subject advisers in the normal consultation between architects and education departments, upon which designers of schools could draw. Use could be made of:

i   Local teachers' associations, for example rural studies, geography, history, environmental studies, biology, art groups. Groups such as these have been consulted successfully in the past.

ii   Relevant curriculum development projects whether nationally based, such as those sponsored by the Schools Council, or those organised on a local or regional basis.

iii   Local and national bodies such as county naturalists' trusts, design centres, the Forestry Commission, the Civic Trust, the British Trust for Ornithology, the Royal Society for the Protection of Birds, the Council for Nature, the Royal Entomological Society and the Town and Country Planning Association, as consultants in matters of a specialist nature.

iv   National educational organisations with specific interests in environmental and other outdoor forms of education. These include the Council for Environmental Education, the Council of Physical Education, the Geographical Association, the National Association for Environmental Education, the Schools Natural Science Society and the Society for Environmental Education.

v   Members of Her Majesty's Inspectorate.

5   The forms used by the Department of Education and Science for local authorities to submit their proposals for new schools do not at present include any defined space for scheduling outdoor resource areas. Until such provision is made a supplementary statement scheduling these areas might be included with the forms. This would entail adding a statement of the rationale for such provision, information about the size and nature of the landspace required and details of special planting and other provision within the resource area. Because there is no space on the relevant forms which positively mentions outdoor resource areas (other than 'playing field preparation' and 'site layout and planting') it is essential to submit such a special schedule and support it with reasons why the areas are as important as other items mentioned on the pro forma. We understand from the Department of Education and Science Buildings and Architects Branch that they would

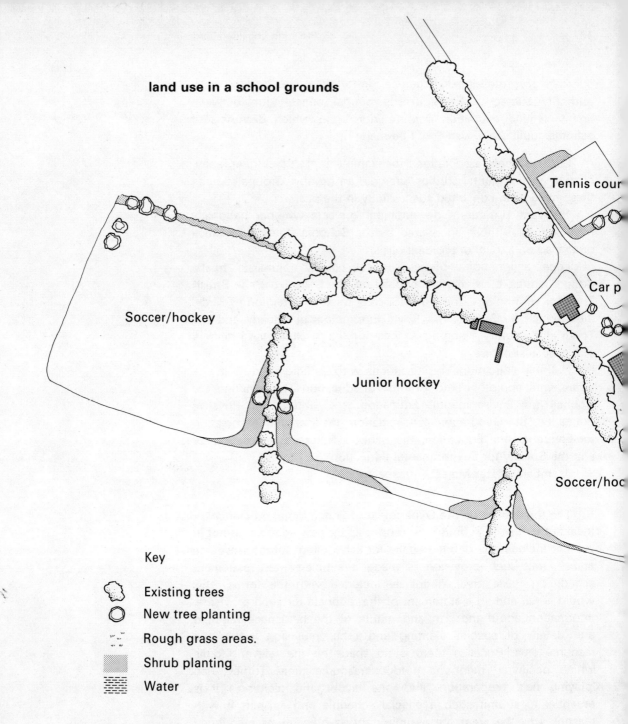

land use in a school grounds

Tennis cour

Car p

Soccer/hockey

Junior hockey

Soccer/hoc

Key

Existing trees

New tree planting

Rough grass areas.

Shrub planting

Water

50m

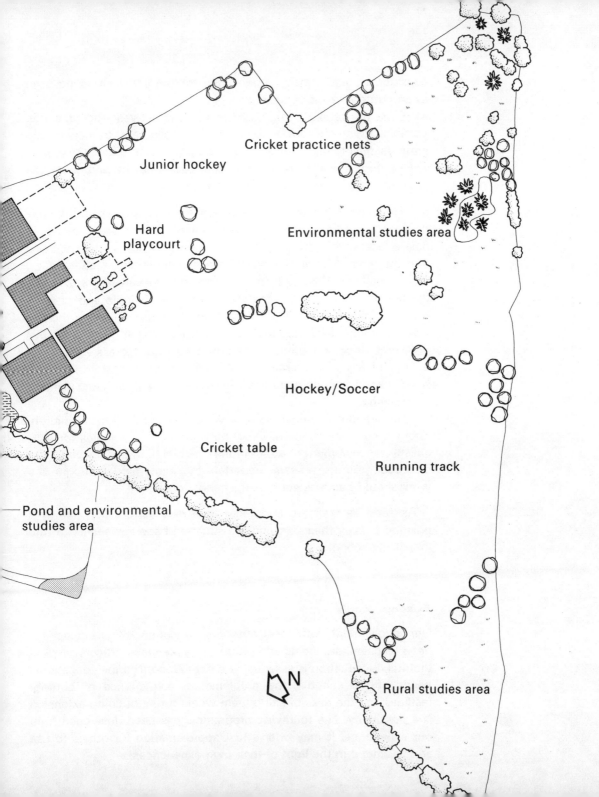

Cricket practice nets

Junior hockey

Hard
playcourt

Environmental studies area

Hockey/Soccer

Cricket table

Running track

Pond and environmental
studies area

N

Rural studies area

consider sympathetically suggestions for the site area to be used as an outdoor resource area.

6 Once the general design has been agreed between the education administrators and the architects, it is necessary to call in the grounds maintenance officers to bring together educational provision, design and maintenance considerations. In particular, the grounds maintenance staff will wish to be consulted on:

a The degree of maintenance of non-traditional areas and the impact of these areas on the upkeep of playing areas. Our experience in past educational work involving the use of school estates suggests that the maintenance of many of the non-traditional features is no more costly than the regular mowing and general care of grass. In fact the maintenance of these features is often spasmodic and of short duration and much of it occurs in the winter season when there is less employment for mowing gangs. Some research into the relative pressures upon manpower of maintaining mown grass and of the upkeep of areas for alternative use is desirable.

b Their role in constructing facilities, preparing ground and planting and sowing.

c The amount of initial planting which should be left to children. There is some evidence to show that one of the remedies for vandalism is involvement of pupils in the use, planning and development of school grounds. It seems important that some participation in the work should begin as soon as the school opens.

As soon as staff are appointed to a new school they are in a position to play their part and the situation becomes similar to that in existing schools.

Existing schools

Our involvement with local authority education officers, teachers, head teachers, architects and grounds maintenance officers showed that full consultation is essential in order to reconcile the educational needs of the schools, the problems of maintenance of outdoor facilities and the risks of siting them where future building extension is a possibility. The following programme has been developed from our experience. It may offer a first approximation for others to use and to amend in the light of their own experiences:

1   The process should begin in the schools with the teachers examining their courses and syllabuses and the needs of their pupils to find where the resources of an outdoor area could be usefully employed. The staff of a school may wish to seek ideas and advice and, apart from the sources mentioned under 3 in New Schools above, the following might be useful.

The advisory staff of the local authority.

The staff of other schools which use comparable outdoor areas. From our experience of developing curricular materials we believe that a good deal of useful information and ideas could come from small working parties of teachers from several schools. These might be set up by local branches of subject associations or by the education authority to examine the nature and use of outdoor resource areas from subject and other educational standpoints.

Publications for environmental education and other outdoor educational activities, a large number of which offer ideas and practical information. These include periodicals, books and occasional papers by teachers' organisations and bodies such as some of the county naturalists' trusts. Sources may be obtained from resource guides such as the Council for Environmental Education's Directory of Environmental Literature and Teaching Aids.

Local information about the above sources could usefully be made available through county circulars, teachers' centres or other local communication methods.

At this stage, the head may find it desirable to appoint a colleague to be responsible for leading the development. His main role would be to help colleagues to find what the outdoor area has to offer them in their teaching and how to decide which features would be most useful to them. These duties, and others, are developed more fully in the following section on management.

2   When the teaching staff have decided on their needs, these should be drawn up in a clear statement of the features they require, suggestions for their design and proposals for their siting.

3   Having drawn up a document about the changes the staff wishes to see made in the school grounds, head teachers will need to know to whom they should send the plans, whether the changes are minor and capable of implementation within the schools' resources or whether requiring help from the architects and grounds maintenance staff. In either case these departments of the authority will usually need to be consulted about the proposals, as will the

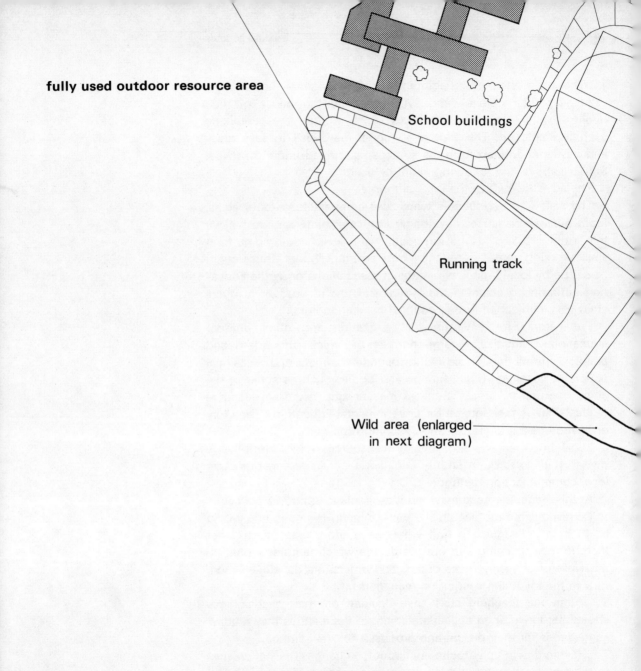

fully used outdoor resource area

School buildings

Running track

Wild area (enlarged
in next diagram)

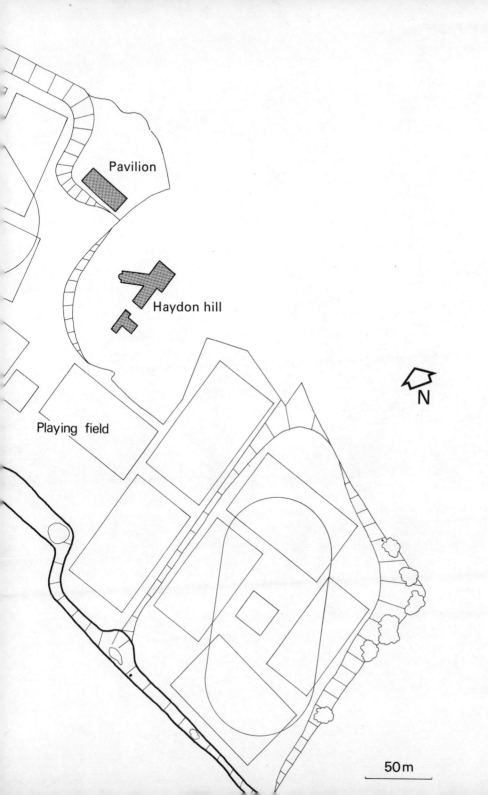

Pavilion

Haydon hill

Playing field

N

50 m

the wildlife area enlarged

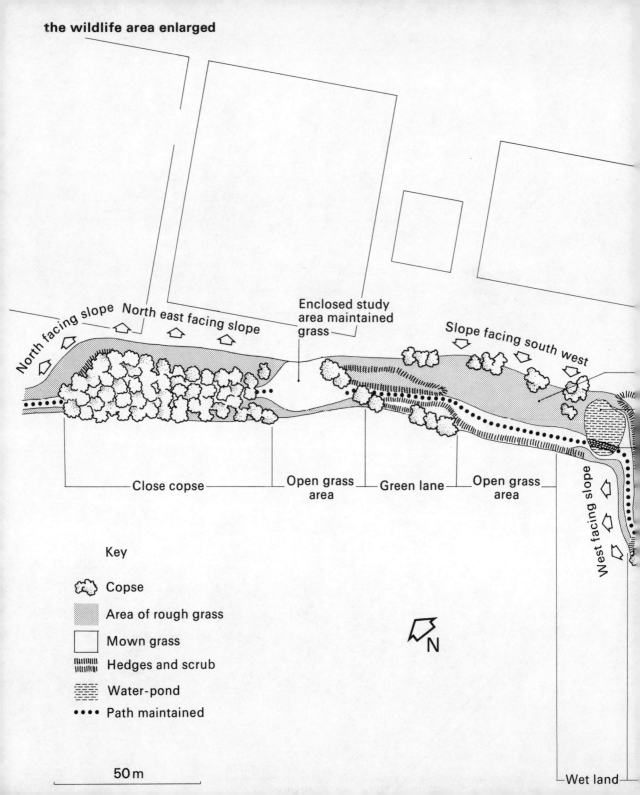

North facing slope

North east facing slope

Enclosed study area maintained grass

Slope facing south west

West facing slope

Close copse

Open grass area

Green lane

Open grass area

Key

Copse

Area of rough grass

Mown grass

Hedges and scrub

Water-pond

Path maintained

N

50 m

Wet land

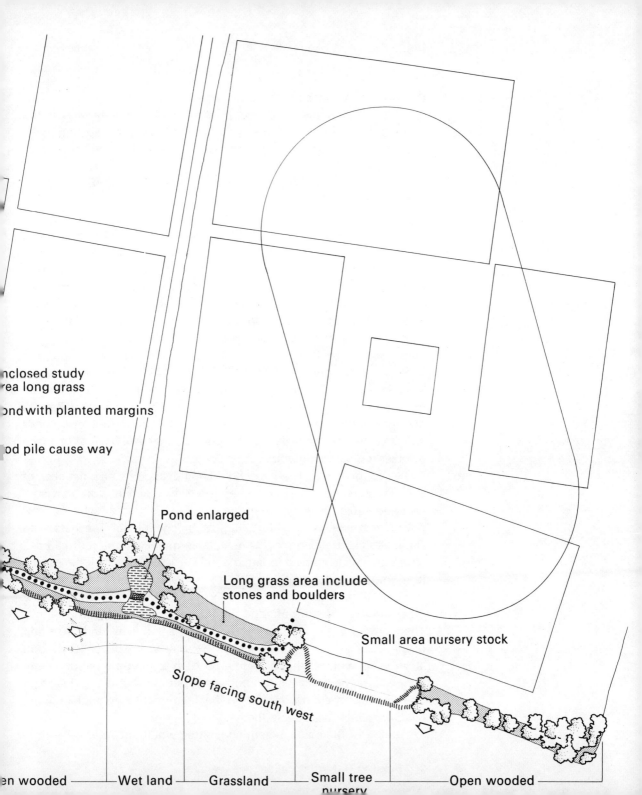

nclosed study
rea long grass

ond with planted margins

od pile cause way

Pond enlarged

Long grass area include
stones and boulders

Small area nursery stock

Slope facing south west

en wooded ——— Wet land ——— Grassland ——— Small tree nursery ——— Open wooded appropriate member of the advisory staff.

4   When final plans which reconcile all needs are being drawn, the LEA's arrangements for financing the supply of materials, any constructional work or additional maintenance need to be settled.

Management

A good system of management is needed if the best use is to be made of the outdoor resources of the school. The analogy between the library and the outdoor resource area has already been made and just as the library is managed so that all parts of the curriculum are catered for and books and other materials are quickly accessible in a usable condition, so with the outdoor resource area staff needs have to be ascertained and provided for as far as possible and steps have to be taken to see that the facilities are wisely used and kept in satisfactory condition.

Living materials are fragile and susceptible to over use and so may have to be rested on occasion lest they deteriorate. Repairs and reconstruction may be needed and from time to time new needs will arise and old ones decline, so that changes will have to be made to meet the new situation.

We suggest that head teachers should appoint one member of staff to be responsible for management, in a similar way that staff are appointed with librarianship duties. In larger schools, this person might lead a small management committee. Teachers with Rural Studies training may have suitable qualifications for this post, although a wide understanding of total curriculum needs is necessary. It is important to bear in mind that management of an outdoor resource area is not a matter of the Rural Studies teacher, or any other member of staff, offering the facilities of his subject to others. The qualities of the manager must include a sufficient understanding of all areas of the curriculum and the way in which colleagues in all subjects work so that he is in a position to advise them on where the resource he manages can be most useful to them, to guide them to formulate their needs and to be instrumental in initiating the facilities which will satisfy them.

The job of the management committee would include:

1   Finding out what colleagues want.

2   Suggesting how colleagues might use the site where they are unsure of the opportunities it might offer them.

It is worth mentioning at this point the importance of exploring the needs of the pupils in their courses to find the outdoor facilities needed, rather than designing features first. There is evidence from existing and past use of school grounds for educational activities that resources have been designed and provided without first ensuring that they are needed. This results either in failure to use them, often making a maintenance problem for which there is no educational return, or in irrelevant activities for the pupils as courses are adapted to make use of these features.

3   Deciding between conflicting claims. This is another reason for understanding something about the activities of the whole school.

4   Producing plans to meet the needs of colleagues. Agreeing these with the head teacher and through him with LEA officials.

5   Encouraging colleagues to use the facilities by offering information and suggestions. This would be a continuing service.

6   Collecting information about the area. In particular a resource bank of information about matters such as the natural history of the site, its geographical features and its history could be invaluable to pupils and staff. The bank could be built up over the years, adding information which arises from pupils' projects and other investigations. Coupled with this, the managers would oversee the upkeep of any labelling which was necessary.

In addition the managers could build a centre of information about outdoor resource areas and their use by teachers. This might include experiences from other schools and from research projects.

7   Regulating use to avoid damage from overuse and unintentional interference with work being carried on by other members of staff and their classes.

8   Keeping an eye on maintenance, whether by travelling teams, groundsmen or special ancillary help. Some authorities make special provision for the staffing of school resource centres, usually developed around the library; the outdoor resource centre likewise ought to be provided for in a similar way.

Some schools already have nature reserves which form part of the school estate. We have been struck by the number of others which have potential areas for this purpose, even in some of the more industrialised counties. These reserves are particularly valuable, as they offer an opportunity for schools to demonstrate that they really care about conservation and are prepared to do more than just talk about it. The management of the nature reserve is vital to this educational purpose, just as it is essential if the conservation aim is to be achieved, because it is through the process of management that pupils will see conservation in action.

Some schools have set up conservation management committees to plan the long-term care and development of the reserve and to reconcile its use for teaching purposes with this. These committees include pupils and staff and also naturalists, foresters, nurserymen and other experts. The function of the committee is to draw up long-term development plans for planting and clearing to enrich the site and conserve a varied but balanced plant and animals community, to decide on short-term and immediate conservation tasks and to advise on the use of the reserve for teaching and when it should be left undisturbed. We see very good reason for the formation of a school conservation corps to carry out the necessary work prescribed by the committee for this would be an essential part of the real involvement of the school in practical conservation. This sort of cooperation between a girls' grammar school and local conservation experts led to the development of the school woodland mentioned on page 76.

Curriculum studies and teachers' courses

The design, development and management of outdoor resource areas presupposes to some extent that teachers are familiar with them and their use. Apart from physical education, rural studies and to a smaller extent biology, there is little precedent for using the land around the buildings. However in recent years teachers have shown an increasing desire to make use of their school grounds, and this has been manifested in the great interest in courses on this matter with which we have been involved recently. There is an urgent need to help more teachers to discover which features would be most helpful in their work and how to make most use of them. It is essential that the new look at the school grounds by the teaching profession, educational administrators, architects and grounds maintenance officers should be paralleled by curriculum development activities and training at both initial and in-service level.

Teachers are aware that authorities can make provision only in response to demand by the schools and to assurances that the resource will be adequately used. They need support from local education authorities and centres of training in developing their expertise in this field. Since we need to know a lot more about the best way to use school grounds as an educational resource, curriculum research might well go hand in hand with teachers' courses in this field.

There are five main areas in which study is needed:

1   Investigating how outdoor resource areas can contribute to the curriculum through all subjects, in particular how the areas can be used to interrelate pupil activities in classroom and laboratory with those outside school, whether in the immediate locality or during more distant day and residential visits.

2   Determining the features which are needed to provide for the contribution described in 1. Apart from the extensive use for physical education, many features useful to biology, rural studies and nature study are evident already from past use of parts of the school grounds for school gardens and nature study areas. Features which are needed by some other parts of the curriculum are much less clearly defined or confirmed by experience.

3   Discovering how the features determined in 2 may be used to provide learning experiences which are integrated into pupils' total education. This is closely linked to 2, for as new uses are found for a particular feature it will probably be necessary to alter it.

4   Exploring methods of educational management of outdoor resource areas. Just as we are learning about the sort of people we need to staff indoor resource areas we need to find out about the nature of the duties of their colleagues outside.

5   The best way of collecting and storing information about the outdoor resource area for an information bank in the school to which all staff and pupils have access. This was referred to briefly above.

Working parties might study the kind of features which would be useful teaching aids and the ways in which these could be most effectively used. Following such work, courses could disseminate the findings of the working parties. Other courses are needed to help teachers who are not used to outdoor teaching and managing field studies activities, such as planning work and managing groups of children out of doors. Others might be designed to help them to become managers of learning situations out of doors, involving their pupils in investigational activities. Many teachers feel insecure outside the classroom because they feel that they have inadequate knowledge about such things as plant and animal identification. Courses which give confidence would be useful by helping them to respond to questions which they cannot immediately answer and by showing them the sources of information to which they can turn.

There is scope for subject specialists in colleges and departments of education to keep abreast of the provision and use of facilities within school grounds and to participate in the general research and development in this field. In this way new teachers will enter the schools with a measure of understanding of the potential of outdoor resource areas and with some knowledge of how they may be used effectively.

Book list

Berkshire, Buckinghamshire and Oxfordshire Naturalists Trust. *Projects for Environmental Studies*, BBONT, 1970

Carson, S. McB., and Colton, R. W. *The Teaching of Rural Studies,* Arnold 1962

Department of Education and Science. *Schools and the Countryside,* HMSO, 1969

Department of Education and Science. *Keeping Animals in Schools,* HMSO, 1971

Devon Trust for Nature Conservation. *School Projects in Nature History,* 2 vols., Devon Trust for Nature Conservation, 1965, 1969

Johnson, C., and Smith, J., comp. *Directory of Environmental Literature and Teaching Aids,* Council for Environmental Education, c/o School of Education, University of Reading, London Road, Reading RG1 5AQ, 1972

Morgan, R. F. *Environmental Biology,* 4 vols., Pergamon Press, 1963–66

Wilson, R. W. *Nature in Your Town*, Crusade Against All Cruelty to Animals, 1970

Index